JENNIFER DAWN

JOY
the
GUIDE

FINDING YOUR JOY IN A WORLD OF CRAP

CONTENTS

Are You Happy?....................................1
Make the Choice....................................3
Getting Started....................................5
You Make Time....................................11
Feel Better Now!....................................15
The Joy Killers....................................35
Clear The Junk From Your Trunk....................45
Gaining Momentum and Confidence..................53
Gratitude and Why it Matters.....................65
Daily Gratitude Practice...........................71
My Focus Wheel....................................75
Defining Success On Your Terms...................77
List of Values....................................85
Reaffirm Your Values..............................89
The Power of Quiet................................91
Clarify Your Vision...............................99
Strategy: The Missing Link.......................111
Eliminate Overwhelm..............................135
The Life Changing A Task.........................143
The Daily Planning Habit.........................153
Me Time is Nonnegotiable.........................157
Putting it All Together..........................163
Final Thoughts...................................179

This book is dedicated to love, light, happiness, peace, ease, flow, and joy. May you have more of it in your daily life.

ARE YOU HAPPY?

When I asked that question an answer popped into your mind without any thought or hesitation.

Be honest, what was it?

No.
Not really.
Sometimes.
I want to be.
I wish.
Yes of course (which is total crap because I'm burying the truth).
Most of the time.
Often but not enough.
Absolutely (because I know that's the "right" answer but it's not really so).
Yes.

Regardless of your answer. This book is for you.

If you seek to live each day feeling more joy, you're in the right place.

If you struggle to find your joy, I want to help.

MAKE THE CHOICE

"*Success is not an accident. It is the result of your attitude and your attitude is a choice. Hence success is a matter of choice and not chance.*"

—Shiv Khera

I WAS FOUR, maybe five years old. We were living in the green house in Las Vegas. I had the white bike with tassels and a yellow banana seat. I loved that bike. I tried to jump it over the ramp the neighborhood boys had set up in the street. Instead of flying off the edge and becoming airborne like I'd seen them do a hundred times, I flopped over the edge and smacked face first into the pavement. I was so angry those boys had figured out how to do something I couldn't do. My father had seen my blunder through the living room window and laughed at me when I shambled back into the house. I never tried it again.

This was the same father who had been getting in the shower with me. I was too young to understand why he was doing it; I just knew I didn't like it. I told my mother. A fight ensued. I stood quietly in the kitchen corner of the green house watching them yell and scream at each other. He said I was a liar. She chose to believe him. He kept getting in the shower with me. I knew it was now my problem and I was on my own.

But here's the kicker: I was still a happy kid. Despite what was going on in my life at home I still laughed. I still felt love in my heart. I still believed life was good and worth living. I chose to be happy, in spite of the circumstances of my life. It just seemed like the most logical option.

I had a choice: I could let my father kill my joy, or not. I chose not.

You have a choice, too.

Whatever crap is going on or has gone on in your life, right now the only thing you can control is whether you let that crap steal your joy, or you don't.

"A journey of a thousand miles begins with a single step." The first one here is to choose joy. It doesn't matter if you don't know how to get there. All the obstacles that might be standing in the way don't matter either. Decide what you want. Not because it's what you "should" do or someone is pressuring you to do it, but because in your heart it's what you truly want.

This book is about finding your joy. It's not lost, I promise. It's inside you, just waiting to be let out of whatever cage you've locked it into. Some of you have not only sealed it away, you've buried it deep in the earth, poured concrete over it and parked a semitrailer on top to make sure it will never escape. For others you let it out of the cage sometimes, but you can't quite figure out how to fully release it for good.

That begins to change today.

GETTING STARTED

"Joy is what happens to us when we allow ourselves to recognize how good things really are."
—Marianne Williamson

We set goals because we believe the end result will make us happier.

When I lose these last twenty pounds, I'll finally be happy with my body. Until then I'm not going out in public.

If I can just make more money, it will solve everything, and things will be purr-fect.

If I can just get my business to the next level, I'll finally be able to relax and take a real vacation with my family and have some fun, but please excuse me I need to get back to the grind now.

I'm so tired of being alone and just want to be happy and in love already. I'm eating ice cream. I hate my life.

Sound familiar?

It should, because there's some variation of this auto-play going on in each of our lives day to day—like a bad song we can't get out of our head.

Do you have a dream you've been trying to achieve without success and it's robbing you of daily joy? Maybe it's the weight that just won't come off or the money you so desperately want to make or the love you feel you deserve but can't seem to find.

You are not alone. In fact, 93% of people never achieve their goals and according to the 2017 Gallup-Sharecare Well-being Index, Americans are more unhappy than they've been in a decade (Gallup.com, 2018). It's the largest decline in the index's ten-year history. People are not connected to their purpose, move through the day stressed out and worried, are less likely to achieve their goals, and are finding little satisfaction from their work and personal lives.

That's disappointing. If you're part of the 93%, it's even sadder (cue the trombone *wah-wah*).

The good news is you *can* join the 7% who *do* achieve their desires each year and live daily with more peace, ease, flow, and joy. That's why I wrote this book. To give you the practical, tactical, rubber meets the road, tangible tools you'll need to start succeeding today.

Have you ever read a great book, attended a seminar, or watched a documentary and been super motivated to change your life? Maybe that's why you picked up this book. It feels like your dreams are totally within reach. Then a few days, maybe weeks go by and you get back into the day-to-day of "life as it is" and very little—or nothing—really changes.

It's such a bummer and so frustrating. Then you beat yourself up, eat a bag of potato chips, and feel worse.

With this guide I wanted to answer the question, *"How do I actually feel more joy in my daily life?"* so after you get all motivated and inspired it won't fall flat because you don't know what to do next.

My purpose here is to provide simple but powerful steps you can take to:

- Shift your mindset out of a crappy place and start living more joyfully.
- Stop feeling overwhelmed, stressed out, spread thin, and connect to the quiet already inside you.
- Quit the busy and start living life on your terms.

This is not a book you read and forget about. It's designed to be a practical guide to set yourself up for more happiness and joy in your daily life, despite all the crap going on in your world.

Too many of us are rushing through life busy and distracted. The trap of working harder and harder, expecting results that never seem to come, is an easy one to fall into. To be truly successful it's necessary to slow down, address what's going on, and build a healthy system for growth and insight you can easily repeat with predictable results.

To get the most from our time together there are three things you'll need:

1. An open mindset to receive the information.
2. A willingness to look at the tough stuff.
3. The energy and determination to do the work.

That's it!

When these conditions are met, you will triumph.

When these conditions are *not* met to some degree you will not see the results your heart desires.

If you have been struggling, you already know this is true. Let's make this time different.

There's information in this book you may have heard before, but studies prove we need to hear something several times in order to get it into our heads. If you are seeing it "yet again" take note. There's a lesson to be learned.

Take in the contents with an open mind, and the results will speak for themselves. If you approach it with a closed mindset such as "*I already know all this, and it won't work for me*" or "*I've tried everything, but nothing ever works for me,*" then guess what? It won't.

Instead, set aside the ego mind for now and forget having something to prove. Set aside whatever crap is going on in your world you can't control. Set aside the negative self-talk keeping you stuck. Set aside what you already know. Set aside any limiting beliefs or stories you've created on why you can't. Let today be a fresh start.

Your open mindset will enable you to absorb and assimilate this information in a productive way that motivates you to *act*.

When you're motivated to act, the next ingredient for success is being willing to change. Let's cut to the chase and address the place where results really come from. They'll come from making changes in your life, habits, routines, thought processes, emotional reactions, and perspectives. You may even find yourself changing your relationships to the toxic people or places hindering your joy.

Change is *not* a bad thing. Think about it. Whatever reality you are living today, you probably desire an improved version of it. To get what you want requires things to change. Resist the change, stay stuck. Embrace the change and move forward.

To make change happen, we take small steps. Consistent small steps lead to success in action.

Pace yourself through the information and do the exercises. Really give them your all. Master each step before moving on to the next.

You may be tempted to dive in and go gangbusters, but instead if you lower the bar just a bit and ease into these exercises gently, you will greatly increase your chances of success and see much better results than rushing through.

Otherwise it's easy to get overwhelmed and just quit. Like most of us today, you're already a busy person with too much on your plate. Take it at your own pace. If you stick with it, your results will be incredible.

I suggest finding a good accountability partner, group, coach, or mentor in your life to help you work through the tough stuff. Do not always try and go it alone. When you surround yourself with people invested in your success, you'll increase your results dramatically.

When we have a goal and nobody knows about it, it's easy to quit. But when you show up each week and have to report progress, you certainly are going to be motivated to do better.

Let's do this…

Summary

You *can* achieve your goals and live each day filled with joy.

Change is *not* a bad thing and required
to get you what you want.

Embrace change and move forward. Resist it and stay stuck.

Pace yourself and do the work 100%.

YOU MAKE TIME

"You will never find the time for anything, if you want time you must make it."

—Charles Buxton

You might be chomping at the bit to devour the information in this book but there is probably a niggling little voice inside your head also saying you don't have the time for this. *Oh Lord… in the intro she mentioned exercises and I don't have time for exercises… I don't have time to pee without being interrupted… how will I find the time for worksheets and tools and personal growth bologna…?*

If you are like most people, rushing through the day, surviving and not thriving, you almost certainly have a time problem. That's not to say you don't have enough time (you do) but there's a problem in how we're programmed to think about time. We've been conditioned to think of it as a limited resource. There are only so many hours in the day. Time is wasting. We're not getting any younger. Get busy. Hurry up.

This is poo-poo.

When we talk about finding your joy in a world of crap, our thinking around time is perhaps the biggest load of crap there is.

Here's the deal-e-o:

Time Is Yours To Master—It Does Not *Master You*

You are *not* a victim to time. You are *not* at the mercy of it. It is *not* outside your control.

If you find yourself running through the day saying things like…

- *There are never enough hours in the day.*
- *I can never get it all done.*
- *I just don't have the time to*_____ *(fill in the blank with something you really want to do but don't make the time to do).*

This is a *choice* you are making.

Be honest. Are you choosing to be at the mercy of time?

Because to get more of it back in your day, you simply need to make a *different* choice. I'm sharing this golden nugget early because you'll need to begin reprogramming your thinking around time to do the work in this guide. Otherwise it will be sooooo easy to procrastinate until later. The time to stop playing that game is today.

To change your relationship with time, the easiest thing to do is replace whatever excuse or self-talk you're giving yourself with a positive time affirmation. For example:

Instead of saying: *I never have enough time.*

Replace this with: *I always have all the time I need.*

When you start putting out a different story around time, almost like magic, you'll get more of it.

Think about it… when you say the words "there is never enough time to get it all done," how does that feel in your body? Kind of small, and hopeless. Instead, if you say to yourself, "time is mine to control today," it opens everything up. It feels lighter, more joyful, and like all things are possible. That's the power of reprogramming your thinking. Because when you believe you have all the time you need, you do.

If you have no idea how to start telling a different story, here are a few affirmations to get you started.

- Because my day is organized, I have plenty of time for everything.
- Being in control of my time energizes me.
- I have the power to complete everything I want to do today.
- I always do the right things at the right time.
- I control how I spend my time.
- I give myself time to do each task at perfect speed.
- I am making time in my life to _____
- I have plenty of time to improve my life.
- I manage my time effectively.
- I identify my priorities and plan time to complete them.
- I make sure the most important tasks are done first.
- I seize every moment in every day.

You don't have to use them all. Pick one that feels good in your bones then repeat it often like a daily mantra. As you read through the options, you'll know which one is best.

Whenever you're feeling pressed for time use time affirmations to reprogram your thinking. This takes intention. When you want to put off reading the next step in this book or doing the exercises, instead, *make time* to improve your life. Even if it's just for five or ten minutes, that's time spent moving in the right direction.

This gets easier with practice, as you successfully reprogram your thinking around time. Write your affirmations down where you can see them often. Put them on a sticky note on your bathroom mirror, in your car, or inside your daily planner. Think them. Speak them. Live them.

Then, watch more time appear in your life. It's not magic, but it sure can feel that way!

There is joy feeling in control of your time.

Summary

You control time, it does not control you.

Make the time to do the work.

Use a time affirmation to begin reprogramming your thinking on time.

FEEL BETTER NOW!

"Now and then it's good to pause in our pursuit of happiness and just be happy."
—Guillaume Apollinaire

LET'S TAKE A look at how you wake up each day.

Joyful?

Eager?

Excited?

Or do you wake up feeling exhausted, overwhelmed, and praying for the weekend to get here already. Does the thought of another day of your life leave you feeling deflated or elated?

The time to feel better is *now*. Not tomorrow or next week or next year when you *finally* lose the weight or *finally* make the money or *finally* find love or whatever "finally" you are attaching to your own happiness.

This is so important I'm going to say it again in all caps…

THE TIME TO FEEL BETTER IS NOW!

If you don't already know me, my name is Jennifer Dawn. I'm a business and mindset coach plus the creator of the *Best Planner Ever* and *Best Journal Ever*. I've grown two multi-million dollar businesses and I'm on track for my third now. I'm happily married with three beautiful children, and I have a horse named Hockey. I love taking motorcycle trips with my husband, doing yoga, hiking in the red rocks of Sedona, Arizona and sitting near the ocean as often as possible.

I live a pretty amazing life, but if you are tempted to think I've never had anything bad happen to me or I don't understand pain and heartache, you would be mistaken. The concepts I'm sharing in this guide are hard won. I live a joy-filled life because I made the choice to do so despite the cards I was dealt.

I don't have a Ph.D. or degrees up the wazoo. In fact, I attended college but never graduated. I dropped out when my grandfather passed away and I funded the trip for my family to attend the funeral. I bankrupted myself and had to take a second job. I lost my momentum and never got it back. I don't regret the choice. My grandfather was worth it.

I believe in education and learning but for me it often didn't come in a classroom setting. I don't use big fancy "intellectual" words and I prefer to keep my ego checked at the door where it belongs. I like things to be simple. Easy to understand. Life is hard enough without all the other B.S. we pile on ourselves.

Growing up I never knew my biological father. Even as an adult, when my husband managed to locate him, he wanted nothing to do with me. The man my mother married when she was pregnant with me and who raised me from birth was a sexual predator. I was abused from a young age and my mother knew about it and did nothing.

My parents' relationship was tumultuous at best and we moved so often I had been in thirteen different schools by the time I hit seventh grade. I stopped making friends because it was pointless. I left home at seventeen and never looked back. As an adult, I went through not one, but two divorces. The second one abusive. I was stalked and terrorized trying to break free from it. I went through a functional depression for over a year and was on food stamps because I had no other way to feed my kids.

The *only* good thing about being at your lowest? You have nowhere else to go. For me, it was the catalyst to reinvent myself, to finally heal the wounds of my past instead of avoiding them and pretending I was okay, to begin changing my mindset and believing there was a better life out there for me. This belief led to different choices, which included taking care of myself and not putting everyone else in my life first. I stopped playing silly roles and trying to be "perfect."

I started to get clear on who I was and my purpose in this life. It didn't happen overnight, but it did happen. And it's still happening every day as I continue to learn, grow, progress, and heal.

I learned *the purpose of life is to be happy.* That's it. To be so filled with light and love that it pours out and all around those around us. The gift is we get to choose what makes us happy. Whatever that is, do more of it.

The great part is that if I can do this, you can too. One of the most valuable lessons I learned through the painful trials of my life is that the time to be happy (and live our true purpose) is *now*. It cannot wait until we are skinnier, richer, or loved by another.

It means if you want to be living the best life you can imagine, you'll need to stop making excuses and start getting into the habit of living that life, *right now*. Otherwise, you'll stay behind the curve. Even if your conditions improve, you'll still be stuck in your comfort zone.

But, don't let the word "comfort" fool you. For so many this is a place racked with pain and grief. Daily stress, living in a constant state of reaction, never taking care of ourselves or having enough money, not being able to remember the last time we belly-laughed… This becomes the norm. What we're used to. Our "comfort zone"—even though it sucks.

To improve our current conditions, we must increase the happiness we *allow* into our lives. Ever heard of someone winning the lottery? Sure, they have some fun for a while. But then they end up right back where they started and maybe even worse off financially. That's because they didn't up-level their comfort zone, create new, healthy habits, or change their core belief system. They made bad decisions, sometimes on a subconscious level, which put them right back to where they started because that's where they believed they should be.

To make better choices for our lives, it's important to expand our joy, change our core beliefs, and stop buying into the lies or we'll wind up right back where we started—back in the old comfort zone of never having enough, surviving each day, and wondering what's the point.

Clients I work with start to see amazing results in their businesses. Then, within a short time, they'll revert back to old bad habits. Why? Because that's what they're used to. They're literally accustomed to feeling like crap every day so when some joy creeps in it totally freaks them out. I'm not judging. I've experienced this in my own life many times, but now, because I can easily recognize what's happening, I'm prepared to handle it—and you can be, too.

That's why I'm diligent about teaching awareness of our comfort zones. Being able to tell the difference between where we are, where we want to be, and recognizing when we start to get what we want it's not a bad thing. It doesn't mean you'll never have a bad day again, but when you do it's much easier to get back on track.

The process of up leveling your comfort zone can be… well… *uncomfortable* at first! The idea is to embrace the improved feeling. Allow it to become your new normal.

Have you ever had anyone say to you, "Why can't you just be happy?" Or maybe you've even said this to yourself… like a million times. I know people who have said this to me. I want to punch them in the face. You cannot just snap your fingers and be happy. There are a myriad of thoughts and beliefs swirling around inside you that manifest as emotions. But what you *can* do is become more aware of how you're feeling, take steps to acknowledge it, and release it so you can then more easily shift to a better feeling, a more positive emotion.

That is within your power. Over time and with practice you can learn how to do this swiftly.

I promised you the "how" behind this stuff, so let's talk about the tangible, practical steps behind starting to feel better now. Let's begin now so you *can* snap your fingers and be happy!

Changing old habits is a process. It requires time and effort. To know you are succeeding, pay attention to how you feel. If you feel just a tiny bit better, you are on the right track. If you feel worse, something's off. Course-correct until you feel better. This might include shifting self-talk, letting yourself off the hook a bit, or telling a joke. It's okay to lighten up.

It's all about setting yourself up to succeed, no matter what, without so much pressure and obligation.

Here's a tool to help you do this:

The Well-Being Assessment
Step 1: Assess Where You Are Right Now—No BS.

Simply move through the major areas of your life and give each a score from 1 to 10. This tool will help you become more aware of what's really going on in your life now.

On the scale:

1 = I hate it, and it can't possibly get worse—put me out of my misery, please.

10 = It's so perfect I can't see any room for improvement—life is beautiful. *Yippee!*

Step 2: Identify Where You *Want* To Be

Once you've scored each section, for any area scoring below 10, ask yourself: What would it take to get this area of my life to a 10?

Write down everything that needs to change for you to get there. This requires you to *think* about where you want to be. Allow yourself to dream big here. Don't worry about how you'll get there, just focus on getting crystal clear about what's in your heart.

Step 3: Start Taking Action

With awareness comes change. After you've completed each section, you'll have a much better idea of what your best life looks like. Then (and we'll dive deeper into this later) you can take clear, focused action to get there.

Now, for those overachievers out there (I can recognize you because I am you) it might be tempting to jump in and start changing everything about your life *right now dammit!* Please don't. Do that and you'll wind up in overwhelm and burnout after a few days… feeling like a failure.

This is a time to slow down, not speed up. When you pass an accident on the street, everyone slows down to get a good look. It's no different here. It's important to take an honest assessment of the good, bad, and ugly going on in our lives and not rush past it.

The point of this exercise is about *awareness* and becoming conscious of what's happening, so we know what's causing us to feel joy or sadness, frustration or bliss. That's how we gain clarity on what needs to change so we can live an "all 10" life.

Take your time with this and really mull it over for a few days. You can complete and use this assessment as often as you like. I'd also suggest completing it away from distractions. Go to a place where it's quiet and you won't be interrupted.

A word of caution: *do not judge yourself* while going through this practice. It will only make you feel like crap. That would really defeat the purpose since the title of this chapter is "Feel *Better* Now!" You are where you are and that's okay. Accept it. Breathe through it. Surrender to it.

I encourage you to take an honest look, because we won't be here for long. With your open mindset and willingness to change, we just need to set our base point to track your progress as we up-level your comfort and happiness zones. There is joy in awareness.

WELL-BEING ASSESSMENT

Well-Being Scale 1-10 (Rate Each Area Where You Land On The Scale)

1 = I hate it. Couldn't be worse.

10 = I love it. Cannot see any way to improve the perfection it already is.

BUSINESS / CAREER score: _____

Doing the work you love. Being fully engaged in your career of choice.

What I love about my work now:

_____

_____

_____

How can I feel happier about my work?

_____

_____

_____

What needs to change to make this a perfect "10" for me:

_____

_____

_____

_____

_____

RELATIONSHIPS / LOVE / SOCIAL score: _____

Having strong relationships with your partner, family, and friends. Love in your life.

What I love about my relationships now:

_____

_____

_____

How can I feel more love in my relationships?

_____

_____

_____

What needs to change to make this a perfect "10" for me?

_____

_____

_____

_____

_____

MONEY / FINANCIAL score: _____

Having enough money and effectively managing it with confidence.

What I love about my money situation now:

_____

_____

_____

How can I feel happier about the money I have in my life?

_____

_____

_____

What needs to change to make this a perfect "10" for me?

_____

_____

_____

_____

_____

_____

PHYSICAL BODY score: _____

Good physical health & endless energy.

What I love about my body now:

_____

_____

_____

How can I feel happier in the body I have?

_____

_____

_____

What needs to change to make this a perfect "10" for me?

_____

_____

_____

_____

_____

COMMUNITY / GIVE BACK score: _____

Being engaged in your community. Doing charitable works and helping others step into greatness.

What I love about helping others step into their greatness:

_____

_____

_____

How can I feel happier with my role in the community?

_____

_____

_____

What needs to change to make this a perfect "10" for me?

_____

_____

_____

_____

_____

_____

ENVIRONMENT score: _____

How do you love the areas where you spend the most time, such as your home, office, or car?

What I love about my "spaces" now:

_____

_____

_____

How can I feel happier in my spaces?

_____

_____

_____

What needs to change to make this a perfect "10" for me?

_____

_____

_____

_____

_____

_____

ME TIME score: _____

Spending quality time to refresh and renew yourself.

What I love about the time I spend to refresh and renew myself now:

_____

_____

_____

How can I make better use of my me time?

_____

_____

_____

What needs to change to make this a perfect "10" for me?

_____

_____

_____

_____

_____

_____

PERSONAL GROWTH score: _____

Developing your own skills, abilities, and purpose.

What I love about myself now:

_____

_____

How would I like to further develop my skills and abilities?

_____

_____

What needs to change to make this a perfect "10" for me?

_____

_____

_____

_____

_____

MIND / SPIRIT score: _____

Sustaining a strong mind and spirit. Feeling connected and living your purpose.

How connected do I feel to myself and my higher purpose?

_____

_____

_____

Am I feeding my mind and spirit each day? Am I feeding it the right stuff?

_____

_____

_____

What needs to change to make this a perfect "10" for me?

_____

_____

_____

_____

_____

_____

YOUR TOP 3

If you could only pick three items to focus on improving, what would they be? Aim to have at least one or two of these in the low scoring areas. Set your intention to feel better each day as you work to improve these areas. Brainstorm two or three small steps you could take each day to begin feeling better—do not overwhelm yourself!

1. _____

Small daily steps I could begin taking:

    1. _____

    2. _____

    3. _____

2. _____

Small daily steps I could begin taking:

    1. _____

    2. _____

    3. _____

3. _____

Small daily steps I could begin taking:

    1. _____

    2. _____

    3. _____

Summary

Take an honest inventory of where you are now. Acknowledge it. Accept it.

Make the time to get clarity on where you truly want to be.

Begin taking small daily steps toward your dream.

If you get overwhelmed, back off. If it feels good, keep going.

Set your intention to allow more joy into your life today—despite current circumstances.

THE JOY KILLERS

"No matter what comes your way, don't lose your joy."
—Joel Osteen

If you are alive, you're carrying junk. No human being is immune to this.

This junk is the underlying emotional stuff that prevents us from living our ideal life and blocks our joy. The natural programming of any human being is to avoid pain and seek pleasure. You see this happening from birth and throughout life. We naturally want to avoid anything that hurts.

If you have ever gone on a diet, you know this to be true. Deprivation sucks, which is why so many diets fail. If they actually worked, there wouldn't be ten million of them. There would just be one or two. Instead, we last for a few days with the pain of denial, then end up seeking the pleasure of the closest drive thru.

This holds true for emotions. Do we want to feel anger, hatred, resentment, jealousy, bitterness? Of course not. It's much easier to numb these emotions with food, alcohol, drugs, sex, shopping, and all sorts of other stuff so we don't have to *feel* them.

Then, because we know these harmful actions are not in our best interests, we experience more unpleasant emotions like guilt, shame, and regret. This feeds the nasty little cycle and keeps it repeating. Emotion happens. Don't want to deal with that. Numb it. Feel like crap some more. Rinse and repeat.

But there is a better way.

Instead of avoiding, numbing, distracting, and hiding from our emotions, we can just feel them. When we allow them to have a voice, it gives them permission to leave. Not only does this feel better, but it unclogs our emotional pipes so the good feelings can flow more freely.

You should be aware of three primary "joy killers." Remember, when you are aware you can then do something about it. Walking around all day miserable gets you nowhere.

The Joy Killers, in no particular order, are:

1. Toxic Grudges
2. Harmful Actions
3. Wrong Beliefs

This is what blocks our happiness and keeps us stuck. If we want to increase joy, we can't do it by ignoring this stuff. Trust me, I tried. It just stays attached to you like cat hair on yoga pants.

In this chapter I've included three exercises to help you identify and eradicate the joy killers from your life. If you've experienced any kind of trauma, these can be tough exercises to complete. However, when you start to go deep and do the emotional work, it will free you from the pain. Do not expect it to happen overnight, but if you commit to your own healing, it will free you in time.

The first step is to recognize how these inhibitors affect you. Is there a negative pattern that keeps repeating, where you always get stuck? We want to identify what's happening so we can fix it for good.

Do not be surprised if you discover behaviors in more than one category. When I did this work for myself, I had stuff going on across the board. As a survivor of sexual abuse, I spent my entire life convincing myself it didn't affect me. After two failed marriages, I met the husband I am happily married to today. Early in our relationship we really struggled, fighting all the time. I could see the pattern—yet another failed relationship—and found a trauma therapist to help me work through it.

I did these exercises as part of my healing journey and found them to be painful at first. After a while, they became extremely helpful in allowing me to move forward. There were times when I wanted to give up or avoid the pain. Instead, I focused on what I really wanted, which was to finally be free of the effects of the trauma and feel better for good.

Today I enjoy a happy and healthy relationship with my husband. You can heal your hurt. I did it, and I know you can too. The goal is to feel better and have more joy in life. This is not something you can fake or pretend your way through. To repair our spirit, we must acknowledge whatever is going on under the surface and make peace with it so we can move forward.

The good news is: *you only have to heal it once.*

As you move through the process, there will almost certainly be multiple layers to push through. It's okay. This is normal and natural. Depending on your personal situation, you may need to reach out for professional assistance. This is not a time to feel shame around getting help. Just do it. Take ownership of your healing and seek out people who can aid your transition.

Your healers might be a coach, therapist, medical doctor, nutritionist, energy worker, massage therapist, chiropractor, or any combination of more than one. Only surround yourself with people who have your highest and best interests in mind.

This is deep work and you should move through it at your own time and pace. Don't expect to sit for three hours with it and be healed forever, hallelujah!

Instead, set aside twenty or thirty minutes every day to sit quietly with it and do the work. Follow your heart and you'll know when you're ready to move forward.

There is joy in doing the work to heal because you are worth it.

Words Have Power

Journaling is a powerful tool you can employ as you move through the Joy Killer Exercises. I was never a big fan of journaling until I came across a powerful version of it, I still use it today in my own life and with my clients. Simply grab blank paper, set the timer for 20 minutes, and pick any area of your life where you feel negative emotion. If you just made a list of all the people who have done you wrong, you might be feeling a bit peeved and it's a great place to start.

The goal is to seek out the negative emotion and journal around it.

You get to feel. You get to rant and rave and curse on the paper. You get to say anything you are feeling without anything or anyone holding you back. This is the stuff we bury and never say out loud. Put it all on the paper. Let it rip.

Then, when you are done, *destroy the pages.*

This is not a journal anyone will ever read. You do not need to re-read the pages. You don't have to justify or explain them. You don't have to go to therapy because of them. Just rip them up, burn them, flush them, whatever works for you, but let them go.

I found this journaling exercise to be so healing it inspired me to create *The Best Journal Ever*. In the journal, the pages are designed to be ripped out and destroyed. We want to give these emotions a voice, but we do not want to hang on to them.

As you move through the Joy Killer exercises, you may find it useful to journal out the negative emotions around your answers.

Joy Killer #1: Toxic Grudges

Use this exercise to take a personal inventory of your own inhibitors. Remember, this is not about judgment, it's about awareness and healing. You can't fix a problem you're not aware of.

Once you know the problem is there, the next step is to take ownership.

Once you "own" it, then you can change it.

- Make a list of every person in your life that has done you wrong. Start from childhood all the way to the present.
- Write down how they hurt you. How did it make you feel?
- Ask yourself, "Am I still carrying any negative emotion toward this person?"
- If so, sit with those feelings. It's okay to feel anger, hurt, resentment, etc. All your feelings are valid. You can journal out your answers. The process of writing is healing.

Ask these questions and write out the answers:

- How are these feelings hurting you in your daily life?
- Are any of those people who hurt you still suffering, or is it just you?

Make a choice. Forgiveness is not about making what they did okay or even having a continued relationship. It's about releasing their hold on you.

Choosing to forgive is for *you*, not for them.

Choose to forgive and free yourself from the energetic and emotional hold they have on you.

Write down, "I forgive _____"

Then say it out loud.

Repeat the above as often as necessary. If you feel a tremendous amount of negative emotions, do the journaling exercise to feel and release them. If necessary, seek professional help to work through and release.

Depending upon how many shit-balls you've come across in life, this could be a long list. I know mine was. Do not let that stop you. It's imperative to free yourself from the hold these people have on you—not for them but for your own health and happiness. Doing it just once or twice probably won't get the job done either. You may have to repeat the words "I forgive ____" a thousand times. That's okay too. It's worth the effort you put into it.

Joy Killer #2: Harmful Actions

Make a list of any harmful action you are participating in. Be honest. This could include destructive eating, alcohol, drugs, shopping, sex, etc. You may not want to admit what you're doing, but I encourage you to do so. This is about awareness so we can change—never about judgement.

Once you have the actions listed, ask yourself:

1. What triggers you to take the harmful action?
2. Are there ways you can reduce or eliminate that trigger in your life?
3. Is the trigger based on a false belief? If so, what is the lie you are telling yourself?
4. With what healthier action could you replace this behavior?

Remember to take your time with these questions and you can also journal about them if the answers are not coming easily for you.

Harmful Action I'm Taking:	What I Could Do Instead:

Joy Killer #3: Wrong Beliefs

Make a list of the negative self-talk that goes through your head. This can be very painful, but I want you to go there. It's that stuff we don't want to admit we're thinking but we are, and it's really hurtful and shaming.

We can't just stop thinking it, but we *can* shift it to something more positive and affirming.

1. What are your mistaken beliefs?
2. Look at each belief on your list. How can you flip it?
3. When negative self-talk starts to happen, what can you do instead to turn it around?

Make your beliefs work for you.

If you are unsure how to identify the beliefs holding you back, here are some practical ways to get in there and seek them out.

- Eliminate all distractions. Sit quietly where you won't be interrupted. Ask the question: How do I really feel about _____ (fill in the blank with an area of your life where you feel challenged)

- Be aware of what pops instantly in your mind. It may not be pretty, but just acknowledge it and write it down. This exercise is just for you and nobody else.

- Anytime you are feeling defensive, or uncomfortable, or not sure *what* you're feeling but it isn't good, take a few quiet moments to ask yourself, "What am I really feeling here?" Don't judge the emotion. Let yourself feel it. As ideas come into your head of why you're feeling this way, write them down.

- Ask your friends and family, "Do I ever insult myself or tear myself down?" If the answer is yes, ask them to tell you what they hear you saying about yourself.

- If you are really angry or upset or having a "venting" session, record it. Just blast away everything that's going on. Then play it back and really listen to what you said. I do this exercise with private clients, and it is always very insightful and revealing of what's really stewing deep inside.

- Pay attention to the thoughts going through your head. Write them down. Do you find that you call yourself names, or are really hard on yourself? Those are crappy beliefs.

The best way to root out these wrong beliefs is through awareness. The objective in this step is to start being more aware. Instead of grinding through the day, we want to begin to pay attention to our self-talk, core beliefs, and any harmful actions we might be taking as a result.

Once you see it, you can change it. This step can take courage, but you are brave, and you've made the decision to change. It's okay to go there, and you will be happy you did.

YOUR TURN

The crappy belief holding me back:	My new powerful belief:

Summary

There are three main inhibitors that kill our joy.

If we seek out the negative emotion and journal about it, we can release it and heal.

We are our beliefs. To change our lives, we must change what we believe.

CLEAR THE JUNK FROM YOUR TRUNK

"My dear friend, clear your mind of can't."
—Samuel Johnson

Now we've started the work to identify all the junk blocking you from joy, the next step is to clear it out. You've been carrying this stuff around, for some of us an entire lifetime, and it's time for it to go bye-bye.

The "junk" are things like lies, limiting beliefs, negative and repressed emotions, dark or heavy energy, bad karma, and anything else in the cosmos blocking you from your truth and purpose. This also includes all your:

Can'ts

Won'ts

Shouldn'ts

Couldn'ts

The Why Bothers

Power Robbers

Doubts

Fears

Saboteurs

They are all part of the Stay Stuck Club. In this club, when we have an inspired idea, they talk us out of it. When we have an important goal to meet but don't know how, they help us "check out" with hours of watching tv or distractions and "busy" work. When we know we need to change they convince us of all the reasons why we'll fail and how it's easier (and safer) not to try at all.

We give that little voice too much of our power.

Think of this Go Nowhere Gang like a 35-year-old child still living at home, leaching off his parents, robbing them of their joy. He complains, whines, finds everything wrong with everyone and is the first one to stop any forward movement or change. He's a real pain in the fanny. It's time to kick the little asshole out of the house already – for his good and yours. We do this with a Clearing Statement.

A Clearing Statement is an intention to release all the crap we've picked up or bought into. Use this statement in your daily meditation, journaling, or even while driving the car, cooking, or taking a shower. It's simple, easy, free, and can be done anywhere, anytime and doesn't require years of therapy. I'm not knocking therapy, and if you are in it, use this in conjunction with it to get even better results.

Like a magician brewing a potion to wipe your memory banks, erase all the lies and limiting beliefs, and create a clean slate on which to create your ideal life – you too can learn how to conjure up a Clearing Statement. This powerful intention will help you:

Rewrite a new story

Destroy limiting beliefs

Clear negative emotional energy

Reprogram neural pathways

To do this, you'll follow a simple three ingredient magical recipe:

Your intention **words**

The **crap** to clear

Where to remove it from

WORDS

Words have power so we want to choose those which resonate with you. Some options might include: erase, remove, de-story (take all the stories out of it), un-create (we create our reality so whatever version of that we don't like we can un-do it), release, let go, destroy, remove, eradicate, delete, eliminate, or clear.

CRAP

The crap we want to clear may include: lies you've bought in to, limiting beliefs holding you back, negative or dark energy in your field or body, repressed or negative emotions in your tissues and cells, bad karma, anything we've inherited or that's been passed down through our family, unhealthy thinking, or bad decision making.

WHERE

Finally, wherever this junk may be hiding we seek it out and destroy it. This might include: your energy field, all time, dimensions, realities, spaces, this lifetime and all lifetimes, your brain, heart, any area of your body which feels dark or heavy, any disease in your body, your tissues, cells, soul, or spirit.

To use a Clearing Statement, first quietly connect to yourself. This might include closing your eyes, clearing your mind, breathing deeply, visualizing or connecting to the Light, feeling/seeing your higher self, or aligning with Source. Once connected, repeat the statement in your mind or out loud to clear whatever needs to go.

You may have to do this multiple times until you begin to feel the "junk" lose its power. You may even need to do it several days or weeks depending on how deep it's buried within you. Just keep at it.

When I'm clearing, I like to "test" the junk first and give it a score. For example, I used to buy into the lie I had to work hard for money. I grew up with parents who worked multiple jobs and they were always fighting about money. I believed if you ever wanted to have any money in life it could only come through long, hard hours at work. I really bought into this story and when I first started clearing it, the power it held for me was a 10 out of 10.

I decided it had to go and began clearing it. I would use many variations of the Clearing Statement during my morning mediation, while I was journaling, even during the day while driving or showering. Within a few days the "power" of this limiting belief dropped to a 5, then a 2 and now it's gone. I will even test the lie again every so often just to make sure it still holds no power over me. If I'm even tempted to fall back into my old ways of grinding out hours for money, I clear it quick and get back into alignment with my true purpose (to be happy). Grinding away is not happy so it must go.

When cooking up a clearing statement use words that resonate with you.

For example, if you think energy work is a bunch of "woo-woo nonsense" then using words like "Uncreate any heavy or dense energy I picked up in my field across all time, space, and dimensions in this lifetime and all lifetimes" may feel a little weird and not hold power for you. If you love energy work this may feel quite wonderful.

If you align with a more traditional modality such as psychology or talk therapy, your clearing statement may look something like "Release any limiting belief in my mindset causing me to make unhealthy choices and blocking me from getting what I want."

The goal here is to create a clearing statement that works for you. We want the words to have power and you have permission to choose the ones best for you.

To get your creative juices flowing, here are some examples of clearing statements I've cooked up:

- Delete, delete, delete anything blocking me from attracting large sums of money quickly and easily.

(This was used to destroy a limiting belief I could only attract *small* sums of money.)

- Release and let go of the limiting belief I have to work hard for money. Clear this from my heart, mind, body, and soul.
- Clear everything in the way of me getting this done.
- Delete, de-story and uncreate everywhere it's hard for me to change and move into something new with grace and ease.
- Let go of everywhere I don't know how to change. Clear this from my past, present, and future energy.
- Release everything blocking me from my highest and best path or living my true purpose.
- Delete, clear, and release all the fear of not having enough from my daily thinking.
- Let go of any lower density energy I picked up today (use this at night just before dozing off).
- Remove all trace of self-doubt and fear I can't achieve my goals.
- Eradicate any vibrational mismatches I'm allowing into my field (great for any and all toxic buggers that have to go).
- De-story the fear of asking for what I want from the time I was a child until now.
- Eliminate any lies I've bought into or limiting beliefs blocking my money and abundance flow.
- Destroy anything standing in the way of me getting exactly what I want when I want it.

- Release anything in my heart, mind, tissues, cells, energy field, current or past lifetimes holding me back.
- Remove anything blocking me from my connection to Source.
- Delete any soul choice keeping me stuck.

When you first begin clearing and feel fear because you don't know how, clear the fear and unblock anything keeping you from knowing the next steps. If you identify some lies or limiting beliefs while you are journaling, clear each of them until they lose their power over you. If the little a-hole is talking you out of taking action, clear him too.

Live From Choice, Not Reaction

The clearing statement helps us wipe the slate clean so we can create the life of our dreams, tap into our daily joy and no longer be talked out of it, distracted or sabotaged.

Instead of living in fear of the "what if" (what if I fail, what if people don't like me anymore, what if I change and I don't like the outcome) we want to make an empowered choice and start living *today* in the energy of our ideal *future*. Clear any and all "what if's" blocking you from that future.

Earlier we talked about the time to feel better is *now*. This is where it really applies. If we live each day in the past lies, doubts, and fears we never get to the ideal future we are working so hard to create.

Living each day from reaction is just winging it and hoping for the best. Making an empowered choice is taking control of what you want and deciding no matter what I'm going to get it.

No more checking out. No more using distractions to avoid doing the work. No more excuses. Instead, clear the negative emotions. Clear anything blocking you from having a life that fills you with joy. Clear the bad habits from your tissues.

Delete anywhere you are choosing to react and stay stuck.

You have permission to let this crap go and find your joy again.

Summary

All the junk we carry around blocks our joy.

We can get rid of this stuff quickly
using a Clearing Statement.

Cook up a statement and use it anytime you
feel blocked or experience doubt or fear.

Live each day from choice, not reaction.

GAINING MOMENTUM AND CONFIDENCE

"Confidence is silent. Insecurities are loud."

—Unknown

You have now taken a giant step into greater self-awareness and have powerful tools you can reuse over and over again as needed. Hopefully you are getting a really good idea of what your best life (all 10s) would look like and have started to identify the crap that's holding you back – and eliminate it.

Great job. I mean it. This is difficult work. The fact that you're doing it, when the majority of the population doesn't have the guts to go to the places you're willing to go, is truly commendable.

If you are tempted to skip this process or not take it seriously, I urge you to go back and do the work. This is the foundation for everything else we're going to do together, and the beginning of new healthy habits going forward.

Now you're probably eager for the next step. It shall not disappoint. We are going to create a **Momentum Grid**. This is a tool I use in my coaching practice to get even the most stubborn, stuck client heading in a new direction. Plus, it also works beautifully for longer-term goals like getting out of debt or losing weight.

You can use this powerful tool repeatedly. Pull it out whenever you need it. The exercise is designed to help you build the right momentum and confidence in your ideal life.

Before we begin, I do need to mention this: achieving and living your dreams is a process you'll experience and re-experience… forever. Unless you're dead, which hopefully won't happen anytime soon, this process continues your entire life.

There is no, *I'm at point A and when I get to point B, everything will be perfect, and I'll live happily ever after.* The joy is in the journey from A to B. When you get to B, you'll continue to expand and grow and start reaching for point C…. which leads you to D, E, F, and so on… forever.

The trick is to master enjoying the daily ride. It's the stuff in the middle that matters most. This may be a difficult concept to embrace. It certainly was for me. I've often felt "programmed" to always be reaching for some point in the future where I could be happy and not have to work so hard. But it never arrived!

While growing my first software company I would get up early and hit the ground running. I'd make a "to do" list a mile long then laser focus on crossing as many things off the list as possible. I took care of my children, but I didn't really spend quality time with them. The clients always came first. Over my health, my sanity, and my soul. I had a dream of owning a seven-figure business and nothing was going to stop me.

Not only was the "dream" a coping mechanism (I found safety in my career and could pretend my childhood didn't affect me and I was fine) I also believed if I could provide for my family in a way my parents never did, I'd be able to avoid the pain and heartache of my own upbringing.

I'd crash into bed each night, completely and utterly exhausted. I had been busy all day, madly crossing things off that list but not sure what I had really accomplished. I did finally hit seven figures, but it took forever and the cost was high.

I finally wore myself out to the point where I just had to find a better way. I ended up selling the company and going through my first divorce. I bought another company, which failed, and I closed the doors within a year. I went from having tons of cash to being $178,000 in debt. I will never forget that number.

I remarried, had baby number three, and moved across the country to take a corporate job. I was the Software Division President for a $54 million manufacturing firm. The first year I thought I had found my dream job and all my hard work growing my first company had paid off. I planned to stay and retire in that position.

Nope. Didn't happen.

Instead, I discovered problems in their software which had been there before I was hired. I sat at my big executive desk knowing, *If I do the right thing and tell what I found my career here is over.* In my gut I knew it to be true, and I considered just continuing to play the game and pretend I didn't know. But in my heart I had to do what was right and try to solve the problem.

I shared my findings with the owner of the company and that was the beginning of the end. They went against my recommendations and tried to "fix" the software, which became a multi-million dollar clusterfuck. In time, they blamed me for the problems, took away the office, and stuck me in a cubicle. I was demoralized.

I wanted to fight them, but on the home front I was also battling an abusive marriage. The emotional toll it took nearly broke me. Then I lost two horses within thirty days of each other. Horses have always been a source of joy for me, and suddenly they were gone, too. That's when I found myself in a functional depression.

Alone with three children, a corporate nightmare job, bills up the ass, and no family or friends to help. I worked twelve-hour days. The nanny knew my kids better than me. I hired a life coach to help me figure it out. It was a big step because I never asked for help. Some of our coaching calls were just her listening to me sob.

But it was in this darkest time of my life that I started to discover the secret to living a joyful daily life. The joy was in the little stuff happening each day I was simply overlooking or too "busy" to notice and appreciate.

The joy was stepping outside and feeling the sun on my face. Listening to the sound of my children's laughter. Pizza on Friday nights. Piling in the car and going to the beach on a whim. Despite all the crap going on around me I found a way to smile. To laugh. To love. To live.

When I made this mental switch, everything changed. I began doing all I could to be in the moment, live the joy happening now, breathing in happiness and feeling truly grateful *today*. Not tomorrow, or when I was richer or thinner or had found the right love, but right now in this very moment.

Switching this mindset is key to not only enjoying life *now*, but also starting to live in the present. The present is where your power is. This is how to connect to your passion and higher purpose. Living in the past serves no purpose and dreaming about a future you take no action to manifest is simply wasted time.

When I was at my lowest, I would take small steps to get through the day. It was those small steps, which began to compound, that I got my momentum headed in the right direction. It gave me confidence that no matter the outside circumstances I could change my life for the better.

The process wasn't quick but I eventually left the corporate job. I took some time off and began consulting. I was then asked to lead a national network of women entrepreneurs, and from there my love of coaching was born. Today I'm a successful coach and absolutely love my work. In my practice, I developed the Momentum Grid as a practical tool to help anyone begin taking steps in the direction of their ideal life.

No matter where you are at today, you *can* do something to propel yourself forward.

Here's how it works:

Any bigger goal you desire can't be accomplished in one day. When you completed the Well-Being Assessment, there were probably a few items that scored below 10. When you figured out what needed to change, they were most likely steps that don't happen instantly.

I wish they could, but unless you're Harry Potter with a magic wand, you'll most likely need to make it happen the old-fashioned way, through some clearing, inspired work and determination.

For example:

- If you're trying to lose fifty pounds, it can't melt off today.
- If you want to make a million dollars, again you'll need more than a day (unless you win the lottery, of course, but if you didn't win today, keep reading).
- If you want a great relationship, it takes work and more than a day. Ask any happy couple.

Instead of getting frustrated and angry because it's not happening instantly, what you *can* do is create a Momentum Grid. On the grid, you'll make a list of the resources you *do* have today that will get you closer to the goal. Ideally, break them down into five- or ten-minute actions. As you move through the day, check off as many boxes as you completed toward the goal. Live in the energy of your ideal future, *today*. Anywhere you are stuck, blocked, making excuses, or procrastinating, simply clear it and take a small, powerful step forward.

For Example:

You want to lose fifty pounds. You might not have a magic wand to melt all the weight off today, but what you *do* have is the ability to:

- Drink one glass of water.
- Eat a piece of fruit.
- Go for a ten-minute walk.
- Stretch or move your body to music for five minutes.
- Document what you ate today in a food journal.
- Clean the junk food out of your desk drawer.
- Eat one healthy, nutritious meal.
- Listen to a ten-minute guided meditation on weight loss.
- Find your favorite recipe and replace it with a healthier version.
- Visualize your ideal body and "see" the weight melting off.
- Clear your mindset around weight loss with Clearing Statements.

Get the idea?

You absolutely *do* have the resources to do a few of these things each day. As you get better and better at the process, the items on your grid can and will change. For example, you get so good at drinking more water every day it just becomes part of your daily routine. Then you can take it off your Momentum Grid and replace it with a new item. Or, you increase your ten-minute walk to a twenty-minute walk.

The idea here is to *lower the bar*, and in doing so, set yourself up for long-term success. If you really want to go to the gym four times a week and work out for two hours, that's great. But if you've set this goal and have been failing to meet it for more than six months, the bar is too high. You'll likely never get it going, so just take smaller steps and work your way up the grid.

Let's say you want to make a million dollars. Sure, you can go buy a lottery ticket, but if that doesn't hit, create a Momentum Grid.

Resources you *do* have today might include:

- Opening a savings account
- Putting $25 a week in that savings account.
- Cancelling a service you don't use and putting the money aside (in your new savings account!).
- Buying a book about how to get wealthy.
- Reading that book for ten minutes a day.
- Cut up a credit card.
- Make a double payment on a small monthly bill.
- Journal on your limiting beliefs around money.
- Use money affirmations to change your crappy self-talk on money.
- Do a daily visualization on wealth.
- Clear all the lies you've bought into on making, keeping, and growing money.

These are all small steps you can take today to move you closer to financial health and wealth.

If you want to have a better relationship with your partner or family or friends, a few items on your Momentum Grid may be:

- Send my person a fun, loving text.
- Send them love and blessings through your energy field.
- Tell that person how much I appreciate them and why.
- Write a quick love note and leave it somewhere they'll be surprised to find it.
- Ask your person out on a date.
- Make an effort to really listen and pay attention when that person is talking.
- Disconnect from all electronic devices when sharing a meal.
- Love and appreciate them for where they are now.
- Visualize your ideal relationships.
- Clear anything blocking you from love and joy.

All of these things can be done in ten minutes or less and can have a huge impact on your relationships. If you are without a partner right now, just focus on falling in love with *yourself* for ten minutes a day and see how great that feels. If the only change you made was to be kind and loving to yourself in all things, it would change your life forever.

Next, create your first Momentum Grid.

I've included a sample grid you can use as many times as you like. You can also build this in a spreadsheet if you prefer to do it electronically. Just don't lose the satisfaction of crossing off a box each day. It feels good and is fun too.

Get packs of those gold stars they used in school and put them on the grid. It's encouraging to see those stars add up and know each of them is a step in the right direction.

CAUTION: Please don't try and create ten grids at once! I know there may be several areas where you are struggling, and it will be tempting to create grids for them all. You certainly can over time, but for now, just focus on *one*. Pick one area of your life where you want to see improvement, (you should be very clear on that now from your Well-Being Assessment) and create a Momentum Grid around it.

You've already brainstormed a few small action items, but you may want more, so try and set aside some quiet time to do that. You may also want to keep a sticky note pad and pen handy, as ideas will pop into your head. This way you can add them to your grid easily.

Keep your grid close as you go through the day or complete it at the end of each day. You can keep it on your nightstand, desk, or paperclip it in your daily planner.

If it feels good and you want to do a bit more, go for it. If you start feeling overwhelmed, back off and just do one or two things. As you take small steps forward, do the happy dance. Celebrate each step as if it's a huge victory—because it is.

Let yourself feel the joy around taking these smaller steps. Never beat yourself up because it wasn't more. As you feel the joy, your momentum and confidence will increase.

You are finally on the right track and empowered with a tool you can whip out anytime you feel stuck.

Now it's your turn. Have fun with it and let's keep your drive going!

MOMENTUM GRID

My Big Goal: _____

It feels so good to keep these commitments to myself.

Tiny Actions	Sun	Mon	Tues	Wed	Thurs	Fri	Sat

Summary

We don't have the resources to make
our dreams manifest instantly.

That's okay because the joy is in the little moments
happening each day as our vision unfolds.

We do have resources we can take advantage of now.

Lower the bar and take little steps. If overwhelmed,
back off. If it feels great, add more.

Small steps in the right direction each day
add up to big success in the future.

Let yourself feel the joy of taking smaller
steps in the right direction daily.

GRATITUDE AND WHY IT MATTERS

"We tend to forget that happiness doesn't come as a result of getting something we don't have, but rather of recognizing and appreciating what we do have."
—Frederich Keong

"Gratitude dissolves negativity. Decide that no matter what comes your way, you'll find a grateful heart."
—Unknown

"The miracle of gratitude is that it shifts your perception to such an extent that is changes the world you see."
—Dr. Robert Holden

THERE'S A REASON for the million quotes and inspirational sayings around gratitude. Without question, this is one of the easiest skills to master that will have a huge impact on your life.

Okay you might be thinking, *Oh blah blah blah, I've heard it all about gratitude, what's the big deal?* But hear me out…

Gratitude shifts your mindset.

When you are in the right mindset, you can do anything your little heart desires. When in the wrong mindset, it's like shuffling around all day in shoes two sizes too small, hungry, with a rain cloud over your head.

To live your best life, shifting your mindset is nonnegotiable. You cannot live a happy life *and* go through each day feeling like crap. It's one or the other. Choose joy.

When you're in a bad place it can be difficult to shift out of it. I get it. These concepts are easy to understand but they can be hard work to implement. I'm going to share two powerful tools you can use to shift a negative mindset. The first is a Gratitude Practice and the second a Focus Wheel.

When I speak of gratitude, I'm not talking about saying "thank you" when somebody opens a door. Of course you want to do this, but we want to go much, much deeper.

Our brains are programmed to naturally stew on negative stuff. Think about it. You can get ten compliments and one complaint, and it will be the complaint that keeps you lying in bed wide awake at night. The magic of gratitude is it allows you to take that "negative" and literally transform it into a positive in your life. I'm not kidding. Any negative can be shifted.

For example…

It's the end of a long day. At the dinner table you sit quietly listening to your husband. Then he begins to complain that you're not really present or hearing anything he's saying. The normal reaction may be to get angry and go on the defensive: "Hey, buddy, if you had anything interesting to say I'd probably tune in for that!"

While those feelings are justified (and you can definitely journal about that later) instead try using gratitude. Breathe deeply and ask yourself, "What can I be grateful for this situation teaching me?"

It may not be easy at first, and if you feel stuck get connected and clear anything blocking you, but if you continue to practice gratitude a whole new world opens. In this situation you may realize your husband is right. Sorry, ladies, but sometimes they are. You were in your head and still connected to the busy of the day and not really listening.

It may serve as a reminder to get back to yourself. Remember, the Universe *is* trying to help even if it comes in the unpleasant form of our partner calling us out. Maybe you've skipped meditation or exercise the last few days because of work projects. The reminder is something your heart and soul *needed*. Like a little gift placed in your lap. Thank your husband. Appreciate the information. Schedule time for yourself and get back on track.

Another example…

There is a client driving you insane with their demands. You've discounted their service even though they never pay on time. Using the power of gratitude, look at the situation with new eyes. This is actually an opportunity for personal growth.

Ask yourself, "How can I be grateful for this shitty client?" It may be hard at first to answer but keep trying. If you feel fear around asking the question, clear it out first but keep asking. There is wisdom here. Once you identify what you need to learn, then action can be taken.

Perhaps it's a reminder of the kind of clients you really want to work with, and it increases your resolve to only work with great people, so you fire them and get your sanity back. Maybe it's validation to raise your prices, which would filter out these types of clients, and this is the catalyst to actually do it.

You're going to feel a lot better after you take action. You can be grateful for the lesson learned, the action you took, and how much better you felt afterwards.

- Use gratitude to appreciate the things in life you already have. Remember, what you focus on expands so when you focus on the good, you get more of it.

- Use gratitude to improve any difficult situation and learn from it instead of feeling stuck and resentful.

- Use gratitude to attract what you want in life more easily. Gratitude is the closest mindset to attraction.

When I created *The Best Planner Ever* I added a line for gratitude because I wanted a reminder to practice it *every single day*—it's that important. Use a sticky note, daily planner, electronic calendar, smoke signal, sky writing, or whatever you need as a daily nudge.

If you're looking for ways to truly practice gratitude, pick up the book by Rhonda Byrne titled *The Magic*. She's the lady who did *The Secret* (you can watch it free on Netflix) and she's written several books. *The Magic* is one of my favorites and it takes you through a 28-Day Gratitude Practice. I've done it several times and always gain amazing results.

I've included a sample exercise here of a Daily Gratitude Practice. Just use this format and get started. Ideally, practice gratitude first thing in the morning so it really starts the day off right. Once you get into the habit you can easily do it in ten minutes.

If you struggle each day to find things to be grateful for, here are some ideas.

- Your home (not being homeless)
- Easy access to clean drinking water (many walk miles for water)
- Hot running water (how easy it is to take a shower these days)
- Clean air to breathe (without oxygen we'd just die)
- The beautiful Earth (our mountains, oceans, and forests are just spectacular)
- Your physical body (do you have arms, legs, the ability to walk or run? Not everybody does.)
- Plenty of food to eat (you'll probably never know hunger)
- Your family (what would your life be like without them)
- Friends (they are sometimes better than family)
- Your work or career (does it provide money, benefits, stability, and/or satisfaction?)
- Pets or animals (without question, I couldn't live without a horse in my life)
- Money (look at all it provides and how much fun it is to spend)

Got the idea? Awesome. Now it's your turn.

It's better to write down what you're grateful for each day whenever possible. If for any reason you can't write it down, you can do it while exercising, driving, in the shower, or any other time when your mind is free. It's better to do it in your head than not at all.

I practice gratitude while out for my morning walk. I count on my fingers ten things I have to be grateful for now and then three desired outcomes. It feels great afterwards, and it makes my walk even more powerful. I'll do this while driving, too, especially if there's something not going so great in the day. I just count my fingers on the steering wheel until I get to ten. This works wonders when really busy or aggravated. Switch the mood simply by acknowledging ten things to be grateful for and three fantastic outcomes. It just feels so much better.

Remember: the purpose of this exercise is to shift your mindset. To live better, we must think and feel better.

This tool helps us get there.

Get creative and get in there!

DAILY GRATITUDE PRACTICE

Write down 10 things in your life you are grateful for and why:

1. _____
2. _____
3. _____
4. _____
5. _____
6. _____
7. _____
8. _____
9. _____
10. _____

If you're having a challenge or working to achieve a specific goal, write down three outcomes you would like to see happen and say Thank You, Thank You, Thank You for each outcome as if it's already happened.

1.
Thank you, thank you, thank you…
2.
Thank you, thank you, thank you…
3.
Thank you, thank you, thank you…

Focus Wheel

The next super-cool mindset-shifting, momentum-building tool I want to share is a Focus Wheel. The idea here is to place your intention statement in the center, and then provide supporting statements around it. When you read it, you should feel really, really good. I think of it like a wheel spinning. As I read each statement my wheel spins faster. The wheel is my vibration. The faster it spins, the faster it raises my frequency to that of pure love.

Use a Focus Wheel for any area of your life that needs a little lift. If your mindset is really stuck on money, or health, or your relationships, create a wheel and read it daily to shift yourself out of the daily gunk and into the mindset that will get you what you want.

Remember: what we put out is what we get back. If you put out crap, you are going to get crap back. Shift your mindset so you put out really great stuff and yep, you'll start getting really great stuff back.

It's simple and tremendously powerful when you truly grasp this concept at a cellular level and begin to incorporate it into everything you do. Anything standing in your way – clear it.

Here's an example of a Focus Wheel I did for myself that gets the intention juices flowing:

Intention Statement: I deliberately create my own reality.

(I was working to accept that I was actually in control of my own life and had the power to change it should I choose to do so. Use a powerful intention that applies to you.)

Supporting Statements:

1. I love my perfect body and feeling healthy and alive.
2. It feels so good to let go of all my junk.
3. I love the comfort that comes from connecting with Source Energy.
4. Nothing is outside my reach.
5. I love having a partner and friend to share my life with.
6. I live in the now because it's all that matters.

7. The perfect financial solutions always happen quickly and easily.
8. I love manifesting lots of money with minimal effort.
9. Every day feels fun, relaxed, easy, and joyful.
10. I allow myself to let go and flow freely.
11. Everything always works out perfectly for me.
12. In so many ways I feel like I win the lottery every day.

To make a Focus Wheel really work for you, there needs to be emotion behind it. Choose supporting statements that feel amazing in your bones. Words have power. Choose ones that work for you.

If you can't get all twelve statements right away, don't sweat it. Just let it come to you naturally.

Whenever you feel your mindset slipping, whip this little baby out and get yourself spinning in the *right* direction.

MY FOCUS WHEEL

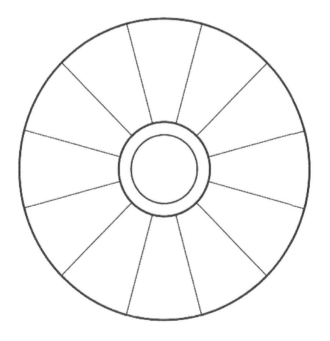

Summary

A grateful mindset attracts good stuff in your life.
A crappy mindset retracts the good stuff.

If you want more of something in your life, spend time feeling truly grateful for how much of it you already have.

Shifting out of a negative mindset isn't easy
and requires intention and work.

To make it easier, use a tool until the process becomes easier.

Any situation can be made better with gratitude.

DEFINING SUCCESS ON YOUR TERMS

"Life will rarely deliver the perfect circumstances to us, so it's our job to make the most of what we're given and use the present moment to push ourselves forward."
—Jennifer Dawn, *Redefining Success*

A FEW YEARS ago I was asked to participate in a book collaboration project called *Redefining Success: 13 Stories Every Female Entrepreneur Should Read*. If you pick up the book, I'm Chapter 4.

What I took away from the experience was the idea of "redefining success." To me it meant I could basically say, "Screw everybody and their ideas of what I should be and let me define success on my own terms," which was pretty *awesome*.

- I could stop worrying about what other people might think of me. The truth is most people are only thinking of themselves anyway. If they focus on you at all, it may be for a few fleeting moments and then they go right back to themselves. So worrying about others truly is wasted effort.

- I could stop playing some BS role like the "perfect mother" or "perfect wife" or "perfect business owner" and just be real with others and myself. The idea of perfection is an impossible myth and the sooner you let this lie go, the better. The best books/movies/stories all have flawed characters. Perfect is boring, annoying, and unattainable.

- I could consider myself a success by my own standards and not by someone else's definition. I consider it a huge success that I've built a business where I can work from home and put my kid on the school bus every day. Someone else may find that absurd and want to be out there climbing the corporate ladder. I would never want that for myself again.

The beauty of defining success on your own terms is that you get exactly what you want while respecting another person getting what they want, too. It's a win-win for us all.

The next step in the Joy Guide process is to start giving some thought to *your* definition of success.

Are you playing a role?

Are you trying to live up to somebody else's expectations such as a parent or partner instead of your own?

Who are you seeking validation from?

Are you living in alignment with your Core Values?

Do you even know what your Core Values are?

If you're not certain about the answers to these questions, they each make an excellent topic for the journaling exercise I shared earlier.

To truly define success on your own terms you must get to know *you*. One of the best ways to do this is using a Core Values Exercise. Once you define your top 3-5 values, you can use them to look objectively at your life.

For example: Do you have a career where you make great money but work very long hours and have little time for a relationship? This works fine if you value money over love. But if your core value is love, then you may find great dissatisfaction in your career, even if other people are telling you, "But you make great money. You should be happy." You will never be truly satisfied when you're living by another's definition of success, one that goes against your own Core Values.

Remember, forget them, this is about you!

If you have spent time defining your Core Values, that's okay, too. Go through the exercise anyway because our values will change over time. It's a good idea to revisit them on at least an annual basis.

When I think about my values before I had children, they were way different than after I became a mother. Your values could easily change after you switch careers, experience the death of a loved one, face a health challenge, go through a divorce, or just get older.

Take your time to move through the exercise. You may find it difficult to choose just 3-5 from the list, but you can do it by taking the time to consider the options.

When I completed this exercise the first time, I found myself grouping values together as a subset of the main one. For example: One of my Core Values is success. When I define success, to me it means wealth, security, stability, and self-reliance. All of those are values on their own, but for me success was at the top. Don't be afraid to group them, just make sure there are at least 3-5 top dogs.

Once you have your values clearly defined, the next step is to compare them to your Well-Being Assessment. Then ask:

Are you scoring lower or higher in areas around your values?

Do you need to make some adjustments based on your values?

Are you living in alignment with your values? For example, if you value you saving money but spend every dime that comes in, you are not in alignment.

If you find you need to adjust your scores, action steps, or priorities in your Well-Being Assessment based on your now clearly defined values, go ahead and do so.

Keep the values in a place where you can easily see and refer to them. When challenges arise in life, or perhaps you never seem to have enough time in the day, do a quick check-in with yourself. Are you making choices in alignment with your values or somebody else's? Again, this is not about judgment or feeling bad, it's about being aware of your choices and deliberate with your time. Once you see what's happening, then you can course correct.

YOUR VALUES = YOUR PRIORITIES

Values are the things you believe in deeply and what's really important in the way you live and work. They (should) determine your *priorities* and are often the measures to tell if your life is turning out the way you want.

When how you live and feel matches your values, life is good, you're satisfied and content. But when it doesn't align, that's when things feel off or wrong. That can be a real source of unhappiness. That is why making a conscious effort to identify your values is so important.

How Your Values Help

Values exist, whether you recognize them or not. Life can be much easier when you acknowledge your values and when you make plans and decisions that honor them.

If you value *family*, but you work seventy-hour weeks in your job or business, you may feel internal stress and conflict. If you *don't* value competition and you work in a highly competitive sales environment, you are highly unlikely to be satisfied with your job. As we've learned about overall well-being, when you are engaged in your career you are *twice as likely* to be living better overall.

> When you *know your values*, you can use them to make decisions about how to best live.

Values are usually stable, yet they don't have strict limits or boundaries. As you move through life, your values may change. For example: When you start your career, success—measured by money and status—might be a top priority. But after you have a family, work-life balance may be what you value more.

As your definition of success changes, so do your personal values. This is why keeping in touch with your values is a lifelong exercise. You should continuously revisit this, especially if you start to feel unbalanced and you can't quite figure out why.

As you go through the exercise below, bear in mind values that were important in the past may not be relevant now.

Defining Your Values

When you define values, you discover what's truly important to you. A good way of starting to do this is to look back on your life and identify when you felt good and confident. At that time were you making good choices? Find examples from both your career and personal life. (If you are the happiest now, that's okay, too.) Write your answers in the spaces below.

Step 1: Identify the times when you were happiest

- What were you doing?
- Were you with other people? Who?
- What other factors contributed to your happiness?

Step 2: Identify the times when you were most proud

- Why were you proud?
- Did other people share your pride? Who?
- What other factors contributed to your feelings of pride?

Step 3: Identify the times when you were most fulfilled and satisfied

- What need or desire was fulfilled?
- How and why did the experience give your life meaning?
- What other factors contributed to your feelings of fulfillment?

Step 4: Determine your top values, based on your experiences of happiness, pride, and fulfillment

- List your best experiences and ask why each is truly important and memorable?

Step 5: Prioritize your top values

This step is probably the most difficult, because you'll have to look deep inside yourself. It's also the *most important* step because when making a decision, you'll have to choose between solutions that may satisfy different values. This is when you must know which value is more important to you.

You can start by assigning each value on the list a 1-10 rating, 10 being the most important.

Then, take all of your 10 scores and do the following:

1. Write down your top scoring values, not in any particular order.

2. Look at the first two values and ask yourself, "If I could satisfy only one of these, which would I choose?" It might help to visualize a situation in which you would have to make that choice. For example: If you compare the values of service and stability, imagine that you must decide whether to sell your house and move to another country to do valuable foreign aide work or keep your house and volunteer to do charity work closer to home.

3. Keep working through the list, by comparing each value with each other value until your list is in the correct order.

4. Ideally, you want to end up with a list of your top 3-5 values.

NOTE: Some values will overlap. For example: Your *top* value may be integrity, which is the umbrella for honesty, truth, trust, and respect. It's okay to have a "parent" value, which then includes some "children" values underneath.

LIST OF VALUES

Abundance
Accountability
Accuracy
Achievement
Adventurousness
Altruism
Ambition
Assertiveness
Balance
Being the best
Belonging
Boldness
Calmness
Caring
Challenge
Cheerfulness
Clear-mindedness
Commitment
Communication
Community
Compassion
Competitiveness
Consistency
Contentment
Continuous
  Improvement
Contribution

Control
Cooperation
Correctness
Courage
Courtesy
Creativity
Curiosity
Decisiveness
Democraticness
Dependability
Determination
Devoutness
Diligence
Discipline
Discretion
Diversity
Ease with uncertainty
Economy
Effectiveness
Efficiency
Elegance
Empathy
Enjoyment
Enthusiasm
Ethics
Equality
Excellence

Excitement	Inner Harmony
Expertise	Inquisitiveness
Exploration	Insightfulness
Expressiveness	Intelligence
Fairness	Intellectual Status
Faith	Intuition
Family	Joy
Fidelity	Justice
Financial stability	Leadership
Fitness	Legacy
Fluency	Love
Focus	Loyalty
Forgiveness	Making a difference
Freedom	Mastery
Friendship	Merit
Fun	Obedience
Generosity	Openness
Goodness	Order
Grace	Originality
Growth	Patience
Happiness	Patriotism
Hard Work	Perfection
Health	Perseverance
Helping Society	Personal Fulfillment
Holiness	Piety
Honesty	Positivity
Honor	Power
Humility	Practicality
Humor	Preparedness
Independence	Professionalism
Ingenuity	Prudence
Initiative	Quality
Integrity	Recognition

Reliability
Resourcefulness
Respect
Responsibility
Restraint
Results-oriented
Rigor
Risk taking
Safety
Security
Self-actualization
Self-control
Selflessness
Self-reliance
Sensitivity
Serenity
Service
Shrewdness
Simplicity
Soundness Speed
Spontaneity
Stability
Strategic
Strength
Structure
Success
Support
Teamwork
Temperance
Thankfulness
Thoroughness
Thoughtfulness
Timeliness

Tolerance
Traditionalism
Trust
Truth
Understanding
Uniqueness
Unity
Usefulness
Vision
Vitality
Wealth
Wisdom
Well-Being

REAFFIRM YOUR VALUES

Check your top-priority values and make sure they fit with your Well-Being Assessment.

- Do these values feel good in your heart?
- Are you proud of them?
- If you weigh any current decision in your life against your values, does the decision become clearer?
- Look at areas in your Well-Being Assessment where you scored low. Was there a conflict in your Core Values?

When you consider your values in decision making, you can be sure to keep your sense of integrity by what you know is right and approach decisions with confidence and clarity. You'll also know that what you're doing is best for current and future happiness and satisfaction.

Making value-based choices may not always be easy but making a choice that you know is right is a lot less difficult in the long run.

Summary

To define success on our own terms we must get to know ourselves.

A useful tool to do this is a Core Values exercise.

When we know our Core Values, we can then assess low scoring areas of our life to see if there is a conflict in values.

Knowing our values helps us better understand why we may feel satisfied or dissatisfied in any area of life.

THE POWER OF QUIET

"Meditation is not a way of making your mind quiet. It is a way of entering in the quiet that is already there."
—Deepak Chopra

TWENTY YEARS AGO, I worked at a frantic pace. Up early to go for a run before the kids woke, then hurry to get them ready and off to school, spend the day putting out fires at the office, rush to pick up the kids, cook dinner, clean up the house, convince the children to get to and stay in bed, then bleary eyed, do some more client work from home, and fall exhausted into bed. My mind would spin at a hundred miles an hour while I tried to sleep before the madness began again.

During that time I sacrificed my health and wellness. I was in a marriage I didn't enjoy. I bent over backward everyday trying to please clients—even the ones who weren't paying their bills. I killed myself trying to be a "perfect mom." Each day was like running a marathon with no finish line. I never took the time to slow down and reflect on where I was going.

I didn't have any concept of meditation. I grew up in a restrictive religious household that taught nothing of spirituality. Honestly, nobody ever taught the importance of having a real connection with Universal Source Energy. It was tow the line or you were going to Hell. Plus, the role of a woman and her sole purpose in life was to get married and have kids. While I knew I wanted that for myself, I also wanted so much more.

I just kept myself busy thinking, *If I just work harder, it will all work itself out.*

Well, it didn't.

Over the next decade I paid high prices in life.

- Divorce
- Loss
- Grief
- Frustration
- Heartbreak
- Death
- Overwhelm
- Exhaustion
- Depression

Looking back on the past versus how I live now, the biggest missing component was taking time to slow down, reflect on where I was, and get truly connected. I never felt "grounded" or in touch with my highest and best self. My purpose was to stay busy and escape the pain, not fulfill my calling in life.

I never had a guide teach me why quiet time was so important. I thought meditation was something Buddhist monks did high atop a mountain; not regular folk like me.

After life put me on my knees and I started the process of rebuilding, I began learning more and more about meditation and visualization. I wasn't very good left to my own devices but found I could really get into a guided meditation. Then, once in a quiet, connected state, I got better and better at visualization, seeing myself succeeding and living the life I dreamed about.

I also discovered the world's top athletes and businesspeople used these techniques with great success. Over a thousand scientific studies have been done on the effectiveness of meditation. Some people you may recognize who practice meditation include Bill Gates, Will Smith, Jerry Seinfeld, Paul McCartney, and Ellen DeGeneres. A few others include:

- Phil Jackson, coach of Michael Jordon (who also meditates), preaches Mindfulness
- Kobe Bryant meditates every morning to anchor himself and control the day
- Jennifer Lopez uses meditation to help her stay on top of her hectic celebrity life
- Russell Simmons, music icon and founder of Def Jam Records wrote an entire book on meditation called Success Through Stillness
- George Lucas, billionaire and creator of *Star Wars* and Indiana Jones
- Clint Eastwood has been practicing transcendental meditation for 40 years.

I figured if people who were achieving at a level I dreamed about were doing this stuff, it made even more sense to pay attention to it.

I also found there were many, many ways to meditate and visualize that didn't involve sitting on a mat. It can be done outside while walking on a mountain trail, laying in bed just before falling sleep, while taking a steamy shower, driving the kids to school, or even out at the barn riding the horse. Anything that helps quiet the mind and get you into a connected state counts.

From there, you can see yourself succeeding in all you do. It is pure bliss. From this state of mind you'll receive inspiration, clarity, and insight. These things do not come from states of stress, overwhelm, and living a reactive life 24/7.

I'm not advocating you now change your entire life, start wearing long robes, and meditating three hours a day. But I do recommend taking some quiet time every day to give your brain a break and find the silence within.

Here are some of the quiet times I enjoy and recommend.

- **Meditation**—time to just be. Gently push out thoughts as they enter the mind. Focus on breathing and connecting to the body. A guided meditation is helpful to settle the brain if you struggle to do it on your own. It can last ten minutes, or as long as you like. A transitional meditation of two or three minutes can be used between projects or as you move from work to home. Simply close your eyes, breathe deeply, clear the mind, and connect to the calm.

- **Visualization**—see yourself succeeding. In a quiet, connected place imagine how you want the day to go. See yourself having a variety of satisfying experiences. Imagine an ideal body, money flowing into your bank accounts easily, loving relationships filling you with joy, or anything your heart desires. When trying to figure out what you want, explore these variations until you find the one that resonates.
- **CEO Thinking Time**—time to plan and strategize. If you are a business owner or corporate executive, sometimes you just need time to think. You could certainly begin with a few minutes of meditation to get quiet and then visualize yourself finding the perfect strategy. Clear any junk getting in the way. After that, sit and ponder. Use this time in any way needed to work through complex projects, outline schedules, map out objectives, or think through desired outcomes. Giving yourself time to simply sit and think saves execution time.
- **Problem Solving**—time to mull over problems. We all experience problems in life and at work. Instead of avoiding them or distracting ourselves, this form of quiet time is about diving into the problem. It's a safe space to explore all aspects from a non-judgmental perspective. Doing a bit of journaling around the problem then sitting quietly to meditate on what came up in the writing can also be effective. All problems don't have to be solved immediately. We can step away, get quiet, and take the time we need to discover a solution.

There is no other agenda here. The idea is to simply take some form of quiet time every day and create a healthy habit of doing so.

Some days it may just be to clear your head. Other days you may specifically want to use this time to work through a project or challenge. At first it may feel funny, but once you get into the habit, it's amazing.

Whenever there's a big project, I intentionally build in extra "thinking" time while moving through it. I'll get done faster and with fewer errors if I clearly *think* my way through it instead of grinding out hours.

Ever had a great idea come to you in the shower? It's the same concept. When the mind is relaxed, we're in a receptive mode. When going through the day crazy busy, we lose that spacious state of simply *being*. That is why taking quiet time is so important and powerful.

If you are cringing at the idea of adding one more thing to the day, I promise it's not as difficult as it may seem. Start with just ten minutes. Eliminate all distractions. Breathe slowly and deeply. Clear your mind and just relax. Set your intention to connect to the Light. Feel your energy field around you all warm and loving. It's totally okay to set a timer.

Use the time to quiet your mind, relax, and get connected. Don't try to solve any problems, just get yourself into a receptive mode so the answers can get through. After the mind is quiet, you can go deeper and reflect on what arises. You can also use this time for a clearing session. Run through multiple clearing statements of anything keeping you stuck or blocked.

Be creative in finding quiet time throughout the day. If I wake up before the alarm, I'll stay in bed and visualize. While driving, turn off any music or audio books and drive in silence. If there's time between clients, move to a different chair and do a two or three minute transition meditation to prepare for the next call. In an office environment, go sit in a bathroom stall for ten minutes and breathe deeply.

A quick word of caution… you may be someone who does not like the silence. When things are quiet, it allows hardships or challenges to present themselves. I truly understand how painful that can be. But I promise it's in your best interest to face these issues or situations instead of burying them. Be brave. There is untapped courage inside of you.

Wounds do not heal on their own. If not addressed, we carry them forever. They steal our joy. They rob us of life and years. They keep negative patterns repeating in life and cause us to make decisions not in our best interests. Use the Joy Killer Exercises and twenty minutes of daily journaling to help clear and heal these emotions. Once you clear out the crap, it will be much easier to connect during your quiet time.

There is no wrong way to do this (except if you don't even try!). It will take practice. Do the best you can until it starts to become an easy daily habit.

To Go Deeper:

If there is a specific issue you want to work on, you can go into the meditation with a focus. Here are some questions to consider:

- What am I really proud of in my life and want more of?
- What do I need to learn about _____ (situation or challenge)?
- In what area of my life do I need to feel better?
- What's blocking me from achieving my goals?
- Are my thoughts and actions in alignment with my vision?
- What beliefs are holding me back?
- What's bothering me?
- What have I been settling for?

Summary

The power of quiet is an untapped resource in life.

When we utilize this power daily, it connects us to ourselves and provides insight, clarity, and focus.

It's okay to be creative in finding ways to be silent.

Start with just ten minutes a day by relaxing and focusing on connecting with Source.

CLARIFY YOUR VISION

"The only thing worse than being blind is having sight, but no vision."

—Helen Keller

LET'S SAY YOU decide to take a trip to visit a place you've always wanted to go. It can be any place your heart desires. Maybe it's a historical city, a museum, a major sporting event, a conference, or a beach on a tropical desert island. I'm going to Finland to stay in a glass top igloo and watch the Northern Lights.

Pick your place and get an image of it in your mind. Can you see it?

Let's pretend we're getting in the car and going to drive there right now. If it requires an airplane ride, we'll drive to the airport, park, fly, and then rent a car when we arrive. Think of the logistics involved to get to your happy place.

Now, get up right now and get in the car and go. We won't pack a suitcase. We won't look at a map, set the GPS, take our phone, buy a ticket, get directions, see what hours they are open, make a reservation, tell people we're leaving, get cash for the trip, take our laptops or book to read, set an email autoresponder, or anything else to prepare for this trip. We'll just get in the car and figure it out along the way.

Do you think this trip will be peaceful, relaxing, joyful, easy, flowing?

Probably not.

There will be a lot of time wasted because we didn't prepare for the journey. We'll be frustrated without the things we need, make tons of mistakes along the way, show up to find they're closed, get lost, get angry, want to give up, curse everything for being so damn hard, and feel sorry for ourselves *Why oh why can't things ever just work out for me?*

This is what we do in life every single day when we aren't working from a clear, thought out, well organized, up to date written statement of exactly what we want our lives to look and feel like. Instead, we have some general idea of where we want to go, then get busy trying to figure it out along the way. We end up frustrated and pissed off, blaming life for sucking so bad.

It makes no logical sense to take a trip without preparation, yet we get up and live our lives with little or no thought and then can't figure out why we are not "living the dream."

Luckily, this is an easy thing to fix. We can create a Vision Statement.

In the Feel Better Now! chapter, we started this process with the Well-Being Assessment. The next step will take it deeper by clarifying the vision of your ideal life. Seeing it as a whole picture. Committing to it so we can make it a reality.

There are many reasons why a Vision Statement is important in helping you find and live your joy. Here are a few:

Short-term vs. Long-term Thinking

The most successful people practice long-term thinking skills. This is the concept of looking ahead into the future then taking steps today to get where you want to be tomorrow. The least successful people (think drug addict on the street) are an extreme example of short-term thinking. They are literally only focused on the next five minutes and where they'll get their next fix. That's it.

If you've ever rushed through a day, frantically checking things off a list, with no thought as to why or where it's taking you, you've experienced short-term thinking. At night, you fall into bed exhausted, knowing you got a lot done but having no idea what you accomplished.

Instead, the world's most successful people spend a great deal of their time thinking about where they're headed. They're strategic, willing to accept short-term pain for long-term gain, and take their critical thinking time quite seriously. As you've probably noticed, their results can be astonishing.

When you spend time thinking long-term, it helps you take actions today that support where you want to go. A Vision Statement puts you in long-term thinking mode. It requires you to think about the trip before getting in the car.

What You Focus on Expands

Visualization is one of the most powerful mind exercises. When you create a Vision Statement and place it where you can read it often, you essentially end up doing short visualization exercises throughout the day.

According to the popular book *The Secret*, "The law of attraction is forming your entire life experience and it is doing that through your thoughts. When you are visualizing, you are emitting a powerful frequency out into the Universe."

We know visualization works. Olympic athletes have been using it for decades to improve performance, and *Psychology Today* reported that the brain patterns activated when a weightlifter lifts heavy weights are also similarly activated when the lifter just imagined (visualized) lifting weights.

There are countless stories of celebrities who were flipping burgers or homeless before the fame and money began to roll in. To name a few: Oprah Winfrey, Steve Harvey, Beyoncé, Katy Perry, and Jim Carrey. They attribute the power of visualization to their success. How did they do it? They took the time to get a clear vision, created a statement or vision board around it, and began to focus on it. What you focus on expands.

If you are focused on the crap in your life, it will expand.

If you are focused on peace, ease, joy flow, and abundance, it too will expand.

In order to utilize the power of visualization, we must first know what we want. Once we know it, then we can see it happening. That's where clarity comes in.

Clarity

A key ingredient in the mindset recipe for success, you must be clear on what you really want so you can become all you believe is possible. Clarity can be used as a tool to inspire you each day, pick you up when things are tough, and a reminder of why you're working so hard.

If you find yourself simply going through the motions, or never thinking about the future, *because you just want to get through today*, you probably don't have clarity. If asked the questions, "What do you want to accomplish today?" or "What do you want your life to be about?" and you don't have an answer, you are certainly without clarity.

This robs you of joy and is a crappy way to feel. Having a written statement solves that problem.

A General Guidance System for Life

The Vision Statement acts as a general guidance system. You can be super organized in planning the day, or set goals up the wazoo, but if you don't have a direction to go in, it's easy to wander for years without getting *clear* results. The Vision Statement is the perfect "double check" tool to measure goals.

Now we get serious…

- Do you have a Vision Statement?
- Is it written down?
- Can you see it and read it often?
- If you have a Vision Statement, was it updated within the last thirty days?

If you answered "no" to any of the above questions. this is for you.

We are going to create a Vision Statement. If you have created one in the past, time to pull it out, dust it off, and give it an update.

Think of a Vision Statement as a blueprint to your ideal life. It can be fun to complete and should make you feel great. If for any reason this scares the shit out of you to put in writing what you want life to look like—don't run from the room screaming, yet.

The process of getting clear on what we want can be terrifying. What if it doesn't happen? What if I change my mind? What if the world found out I have no idea what I really want? What if I fail? What if all my bullshit excuses for why I'm unhappy won't apply now? What if, what if, what if…?

Take a deep breath. Now another one. Clear all those fears, doubts, and what if's. I promise it will be okay.

Taking a trip without a clear plan is *insane*. Going through life without one is too. We don't have to start with a trip across the world, we can begin with a trip across town. If this exercise creates fear or any kind of block within you, journal about it and let it go.

Start with the question, "Why am I afraid to do this?" or "What's blocking me?" and then let whatever answers present flow out on the paper. Be gentle with yourself. It may take several days of journaling to work through the crap. Stick with it. Once you clear it, then continue with creating the Vision Statement.

If you don't know what you want your life to look like right away, that is totally okay. Start with more general statements that feel good to you. For example:

I own a beautiful home in _____.

I feel at peace and safe in my home.

I cherish deep and meaningful relationships with _____.

I live each day feeling joy, peace, and ease.

I love spending time doing _____.

My career (or business) is growing.

I allow ample money to flow to me daily.

I live intentionally in alignment with my Core Values (list them).

I enjoy perfect health.

I have endless energy.

I get a good night's sleep and wake every day feeling rested and alive.

I am safe.

I enjoy perfect love with the partner of my choice.

If you find yourself getting stuck on the details, just go broader. For example, you can't figure out if your dream car should be red or blue, if you'll pay in cash or have a car payment, who will criticize you for owning the car, where you'll park it to keep it safe, how much will the insurance knock you back, and so on… instead go with something like:

I am driving my dream car. While driving I feel successful and abundant. My life rocks.

It's important to feel good here. Details can bog us down or trying to figure out the "how" it will happen. Don't worry about any of that now. Just focus on the final outcome. Remember the dream trip we want to take? That trip is your life. Think about how you want it to feel, the amazing experiences you want to have, all the things that will make it great and worth the effort.

I've included an exercise to craft your Vision Statement. There are starter questions to get your creative juices flowing. Feel free to add more questions as you go along. Set aside at least one hour of quiet time to work on this without distractions. Once the first draft is complete, sleep on it and revisit it for five or ten minutes every day over the course of a week.

Take as much time as you need. I've had clients who took six months to create a Vision Statement. I'd prefer it take six months to complete instead of going an entire lifetime without it.

New ideas about your vision may pop into your mind during the day. Write them down and keep updating until you've gotten to a place where your statement feels good and solid.

Here's the thing… a Vision Statement is never really done, unless you're dead. If you're alive, breathing, growing, and expanding, your Vision Statement should be doing the same with you. Ideally, revisit and update monthly.

This is a work in progress, just like you, so work at your own pace and take the time you need to think it through. Don't try and be perfect the first time out of the gate.

Your Vision Statement

This exercise will take time and energy. Schedule quiet, uninterrupted time to work on it. The goal here is clarity on your life. What do you want *your* trip to look and feel like?

> **Let's close our eyes and take a deep breath. Imagine for a moment you are floating up above in the clouds. As you look down at yourself and your life, in your hand appears a magic wand. You can wave this wand and create any life you desire. As you wave the wand, your most joyful life begins to appear below. Now write down what it looks like. Describe how it feels.**

Dream big. Let the thoughts flow freely as you jot down the loftiest, most exciting picture of your life. The best stories start with an impossible dream that was pursued by someone who was certain they could make it come true. Be as specific as possible and write in the present tense, as if it's happening now.

Shoot for about one page in length. A Vision Statement should be more than a paragraph, but not a novel.

After you have written down the contents of your heart, go a little deeper and ask yourself the questions below. If you are not sure where to start and are staring at a blank page, start with these questions to get the gears turning.

Then, in paragraph form, you can turn your answers into a narrative. Do not simply write an answer to each question and leave it at that. The questions are meant to stimulate your imagination for the vision of your life.

What is your business doing or what does your career look like?
How much is your salary?
How much money would it take for you to feel financially at peace?
What does an ideal day look like for you?
How do you feel about your work? The people you work with? The clients you serve?
What does your home life look like?
What kind of relationships are you having?
How is your health?
What's your fitness level?
How much energy do you have to live each day fully?
Are you doing charitable works or helping others step into greatness?
How are you spending your free time?
Are you taking any trips? What experiences are you having?
What are you doing socially with family and/or friends?
How does your life feel?

After you have completed a first draft of your Vision Statement, read it every day for a week making any changes, updates, or deletions as you see fit. The more you can incorporate your vision into your daily routine, the better.

Keep your vision in a place that's easily accessible. Read it often and share with your team, family, or friends. Use it as a source of inspiration to keep you focused and motivated.

Remember: What you put out is what you get back.

When you read the statement and visualize yourself accomplishing every part of it you begin to put out something powerful: your heart's deepest desire.

Keep the faith, be brave, and keep putting it out there. Then, buckle up. Pay attention to what comes back and let the fun begin.

Optional: Vision Board

A Vision Board is a picture of your ideal life (versus the Vision Statement, which is written). This is a great option if you're a more visual person or want to give your statement extra emotional strength.

A Vision Board should focus on how you want to feel, not just on things you want. Of course, it's great to include material items, but the more feeling you can put behind it, the more quickly you can make it a reality.

Do you want to feel loved and appreciated, maybe successful, or that you provide tremendous value to your clients? Pair words and images on your Vision Board to convey how your ideal life feels.

Many people enjoy cutting pictures out of magazines. I will Google specific images I'm looking for, print, cut, and paste. Make your board your own. Don't try to live another person's life.

The board can be big, on poster board, or small to fit on the pages of a daily planner. Inside *The Best Planner Ever* the first pages are blank and designed for a Vision Statement and Board. This puts your dreams right at your fingertips before planning each day.

A vision board only works if you use it. Pair it with clearing statements to unblock anything hold you back, then quiet time "seeing" it happen.

Summary

You wouldn't take a trip without planning and preparation. Life is no different.

A written Vision Statement is an effective tool for being crystal clear on your ideal life.

If you feel fear or blocked around creating one, journal about it to clear out any crap.

Go broader to avoid getting bogged down in the details.

Reading the Vision Statement should feel amazing. Keep working on it until it does.

Read and align with your vision daily. See it happening.

STRATEGY: THE MISSING LINK

"Our goals can only be reached through the vehicle of a plan. There is no other route to success."

—Pablo Picasso

TRUTH TIME.

It makes my head hurt to think about all the "goal" systems out there... SMART goals, OKR (objectives and key results), 10x, Big Hairy Audacious Goals, Structured & Measured Goals, Just One Thing a Day Goals, the 12-Week Year, the 90-Day Year, the 3x4 system, Push Goals, and on and on and on and on...

Is your head hurting now too?

There are so many options available, all good intentioned. If you are seeing results with a particular system by all means stick with it. We do not want to fix anything that is not broken here.

If you find yourself a bit lost in the whole setting and achieving goals thing or even asking yourself, "Why in the hell do I need goals anyway?" maybe I can help.

First, let's take it back to basics. What is a goal anyway? It's defined as "the object of a person's ambition or effort; an aim or desired result."

That's it. A goal is simply proof you got what you wanted.

If we go back to the trip we're taking, not the insane one where we don't prepare a thing, but the one where we've spent time getting clear on where we want to go, on that trip when you get in the car, the first thing you do is set the GPS if you don't know exactly how to get there. As you drive along, you'll pass things and that's how you know you're on the right track. *There's a gas station on the right, yep, I just passed the McDonalds, I've got two more stoplights and then the destination is on the left. Yippee I made it!*

Goals are those markers along the way letting us know we're on the right track. It's that simple. Making it more complicated is just asking for trouble.

If you're struggling to get the kind of results you want in life, it's time to embrace the process of setting and achieving goals. If you already have a process you love and it's working for you, awesome. Stick with it. If not, I'm going to provide some options around goal setting. It's still up to you to figure out what works for you and embrace it.

You have permission to play around with this. Mix it up and find what meets your exact needs. Most pre-made "systems" are not a perfect fit for everybody. They might be a perfect fit for the person who designed them but need a little adjusting to work for you.

That's okay. Just keep the fundamentals and experiment with the rest. What I've tried to provide is gentle structure, just enough to give you a clear picture of how it works but enough wiggle room to customize it for your own needs. Let's dig in…

No matter what terminology, time segments, or fancy names they go by, all the "systems" out there for setting and achieving goals come down to three basic steps:

- **Get Clear** on what you want to achieve.
- **Make a Plan** of action to accomplish it.
- **Do The Work** to make it happen.

That's it.

In previous chapters you completed the Well-Being Assessment, determined your Core Values, and created a Vision Statement for your life. These are all steps toward **Getting Clear**.

It's your choice to do all or just one of these exercises. Each will provide you with clarity from a slightly different perspective. If you half-assed the Well-Being Assessment and skipped the rest, you might get a little clarity. If you dived into each exercise and gave it 100% you may be feeling tremendous clarity. The more time and effort applied here, the greater the results.

It feels good to know exactly where you are, who you are, and where you want to go. There is joy in clarity.

The next step is to make a plan, and this is the step most people skip right on over. If you ever set a New Year's Resolution to lose weight, went right out and signed up for a gym membership, then found yourself sitting on the couch in February eating your emotions and trying to figure out how to cancel the membership without anyone knowing about it you've experienced the frustration of not making a plan.

You had a burst of determination, set a goal, and got busy taking action. You are not alone. This is what the majority of people do. I did it for years too. You don't even get a badge or anything for being in the I Suck at Goals Club.

There is, however, a better way and it involves one magical ingredient called **Strategy**.

The "official" definition of strategy is a plan of action designed to achieve a major or overall aim. My definition of strategy is slow the hell down and taking time to think it through before killing yourself with action.

The reason you need strategy is because without it you are relying on willpower alone to achieve a goal. While willpower is a vital system crucial in helping us do many important things, as you have almost certainly experienced, it can be a fickle beast.

Willpower is strongest in the morning (yes, it's scientifically proven) and as the day goes along, it naturally declines. At times of stress or exhaustion our willpower takes a hit and that's when we enter into the land of "I just don't care" and our goals and best intentions go flying out the window. *Bye-bye!* You may have experienced this when you start the day fresh and ready to tackle the world, but as the day continues, you get more worn down and end up falling off the wagon.

A much better system to rely on is **Preparation and Planning**. When you make the time to prepare your action steps and plan when they will occur, your chances of success increase dramatically.

This does not mean every day will be perfect. But if you get off track, you have a very clear path back to the land of forward progress. Plus, if you determine a certain action isn't working, you can quickly pivot to a new strategy.

Yes, that's right. You will have to perfect the art of pivoting, aka Plan B. Not everything you try will work out as expected, so you'll be required to (*gasp!*) change.

Look out, it's getting real now…

Committing to more joy in your life also means allowing in some peace, ease, and flow. You can't have ease and flow walking around rigid all day with a stick up the butt refusing to change your ways, making excuses, blaming the "system" for your failure, and being a general pain in the ass. To find more joy, calm, and comfort will require letting down your guard, forgiving yourself, releasing some shit, and chilling the fuck out.

Your life and joy are too important to exist in a constant state of stress and overwhelm over goals.

Instead, you'll need to take it down a notch and breathe.

But I'm not leaving you totally unprepared for how to do this.

- You now know how to *journal* the crap out and let it go with a clearing statement. Use this tool anytime the going gets rough. If you're mad about having to change, feeling blocked on your goals, trying to understand why you procrastinate, beating yourself up, working to change a limiting belief, or anything else you need a safe space to work through, write it out.

- You have the power of a daily *gratitude practice* to shift your mindset. When challenges arise (like having to change or switch to Plan B) you can now pull out the lesson to be learned. Look at things with a different perspective. Shorten your learning curve or begin seeing how a chain of events links like a big glorious universal connect-the-dots picture.

- You understand the power of **quiet**. How success comes through stillness. The different kinds of meditation, visualization, and thinking spaces. Plus, with your new programming around time, how to carve out the moments you need to just be silent.

These tools come together to serve you in any way of your choosing. Choose to use them.

They will be key as you work through the strategy behind your goals.

Why Strategy?

When we talk strategy, we are simply making a plan of action to achieve our goals. There is nothing else more complicated going on here. It's just a plan, man.

You'll see there may be crucial resources like time, money, or skills we need to acquire *first* before we can accomplish the goal. It's about getting clear on the approach before we just get busy doing stuff. You can accomplish every goal you set if you invest the time up front to build a solid game plan.

Now, every good plan also needs a timeframe. Without question, working within a smaller period can be easier, less stressful, and is proven to get better results. Studies show that when you set a goal past six months, your chances of success drop to only 46%. There are some goals, however, where we need to enlist a longer term, some are even for a lifetime. This is the case for health and wellness, money, and love. You don't just get healthy once then never have to deal with it again. It lasts forever.

Take our losing weight analogy. You want to drop weight so you set a ninety-day goal to drop thirty pounds. You suck it up for ninety days and drop the excess poundage, but then what happens? You come off the diet so deprived and exhausted you spend the next ninety days gaining it all back, maybe even a little extra just for good measure. *What the $#%&...?!!*

Instead, it would be a much better plan to permanently change our eating and lifestyle choices over a longer term to see lasting results, instead of ping-ponging back and forth in the viscous cycle of short-term goal, setback, short-term goal, setback, short-term goal, setback, give up, cry.

Instead, take the time to make a plan and identify healthy eating and exercise habits that actually feel good to do and reward yourself for doing them. Not only is it more fun, you don't feel deprived and are much more likely to stick with it long past ninety days. That's what's needed to experience steady forward progress in a life that just keeps feeling better and better. When you feel better, you have more joy.

For example, you might use a Momentum Grid and set a thirty-day goal to drink an extra glass of water every day, replace one sugary snack with a piece of fruit, move your body to music five minutes a day, and clear anything blocking you with visualization. That's it. It might feel like you aren't doing enough at first, but this is the part where you set yourself up for success by lowering the bar.

If it's easy, you're much more likely to do it. If you love dancing around to music it'll be fun. Because it's easy and fun, you'll naturally end up doing more. You might love moving your body so much that five minutes becomes twenty by the end of the thirty days and it just happened without any effort at all. The next month, you notch it up a bit more, always keeping your progress easy and fun. There is joy in forward momentum.

Here's an example of what the strategy for this weight loss goal may look like using the three fundamentals for achieving goals:

#1 Get Clear

I want to lose weight in a way that feels good to me. I love developing permanent healthy habits for eating and exercise that are easy to maintain. I want to enjoy the ride of getting healthy. I see myself succeeding and getting healthier and stronger every day. It feels so gooooood...

I release all the lies and limiting beliefs on why I couldn't lose weight before. I de-story and un-create anything blocking me from my ideal body and perfect health.

I'm at a six for health and to get to a ten I need to lose thirty pounds, maintain a regular exercise routine, stop eating my emotions, and eliminate sugar and dairy from my diet. For me, that feels perfect.

#2 Make a Plan

Instead of trying to all this in thirty deprived and miserable days, I'm going to stretch it out over the next six months. Taking the pressure off myself feels amazing. Through this process, when I feel stressed and pressured, I commit to lowering the bar and giving myself a break. I'm going to write a letter to myself so I can read it when times get tough and remember my commitment.

- Month 1: I'll use a Momentum Grid to start moving my body to music five minutes a day (which I love). I'll build a fun playlist on my phone so the music is queued up and ready to go. I'll set a reminder and block the time on my calendar daily. I'll not deprive myself of any foods I love eating, instead I will make a point to add nutrition to my diet each day. I will eat something green (that's not candy) daily and an apple each day. This is my favorite fruit so it will be easy.
- *Monthly Focus Goal:* Start moving. Add nutrition.
- Month 2: I'll research and sign up for a 5k race. I'll find a six-week training schedule for beginners. I used to run years ago and I loved it. A 5k will be a great goal to set and achieve. I'll call Beth and tell her I'm

ready to start running again. She's been harassing me for years and will make a perfect accountability partner. I will block out the time in my calendar. The training is only for thirty minutes three times a week and feels easy and doable. I will add additional nutrition each day with a glass of raw green juice. I will create a Focus Wheel on health and look at it every day.

- *Monthly Focus Goal:* Bring the joy of running back into my life. Add nutrition.

- Month 3: I gained this extra weight because I'm in a toxic relationship with my work. I know it's not good for me and I will take steps to break free. This month I will update my resume and hire a career coach to help me move forward. I will replace my favorite snack of potato chips with raw nuts. I'll commit to 21 days of a gratitude practice (ten minutes a day) around finding the perfect career.

- *Monthly Focus Goal:* Take steps to find a new career. Add gratitude. Keep going on exercise and nutrition.

- Month 4: I ran my first 5k in years and it felt amazing. I'm signing up for another one and my goal will be to beat my time by ten seconds or more. I will find and apply to ten new jobs this month. I'm ready to start eliminating dairy from my diet. I will find healthy substitutions for my favorite dairy products, so I don't feel like I'm missing out. I will update my Vision Board.

- *Monthly Focus Goal:* Apply for new jobs. Start eliminating dairy. Keep training.

- Month 5: I am not sure exactly where I'll be this month so I will take quiet time to reflect and course correct as necessary. I'll update my Well-Being Assessment and evaluate my progress. I will continue to apply for new jobs. I will take the two weeks of vacation I have stored up and go somewhere fun and make a point to enjoy my life. While on vacation I'll take extra quiet time to meditate and visualize.

- *Monthly Focus Goal:* Relax, recharge, and reflect. Take a Vacation. Maintain nutrition and exercise goals even while on vacation.

- Month 6: I'm in a new career and it feels wonderful. I'm less stressed and finding so much more joy in the day than I ever felt before. I'm ready to make one meal each day entirely raw, live, living foods. I'm going to find one 5k each month for the next three months and sign up for them.

- *Monthly Focus Goal:* Be in a new job. Make one meal a day entirely raw. Improve 5k time.

- Emergency Action Plan: When the shit hits the fan and I want to eat my emotions, instead I will journal and clear. I will not deprive myself, but I will make an effort to deal with the emotions before making a decision about what to eat. As I move through this career change, I will reach out to my coach and ask for help when I need it instead of suffering alone and beating myself up. I will read my Vision Statement daily and create a Focus Wheel when I need an extra boost. I will use the power of gratitude to enjoy my journey and seek joy daily. This is my plan. If things change, I will change too. I commit to health and well-being. Let's do this.

#3 Do The Work

Now that the plan is clear, I simply execute. I've done the work to think it through. I have an accountability partner and coach to support me. I have tools like journaling, Focus Wheels, and gratitude to shift my mindset. If I get stuck, I create a Momentum Grid. I've lowered the bar and set myself up for long-term success. This is in perfect alignment with my vision.

The above is an example of what your strategy may look like. Remember, we are all different. Some may want to spend more time flushing out the details and for others a monthly focus goal may be enough.

NOTE: Don't try and figure out every detail down to the gnat's ass. It can easily turn into an exercise in frustration. Just go as deep as necessary to have a clear picture of your goals each month. Then, allow yourself time and space to work it out.

If you completed any of the Joy Killer exercises you will have a good idea of what is blocking or stopping you. Build these into your strategy—they will come up. By thinking through what you'll do ahead of time, you'll be better prepared to deal with it when it happens. Don't expect perfection the first time out of the gate. Give yourself permission to screw up, then get back on track. Over time it will get easier.

One thing I want you to notice about the above example: getting clear and taking action are relatively small. They only require a few sentences to describe. While making a plan is enormous in comparison. It takes some work and brain power to do this correctly. That's why so many people skip over it. However, if you do the "thinking" work before getting busy, when it's time to take action it will fall out almost without any effort at all.

You can use this strategy to meet any goal your heart desires. Achieving goals does not need to be restrictive, demanding, grueling, tough, arduous, or difficult. You can choose to make them fun, playful, lively, humorous, and joyful.

It's entirely possible to meet any big goal for yourself like paying off debt, running a 5k, or improving the cash flow in your business by taking super-small, teenie-weenie steps every day. Making it so easy on yourself it almost doesn't feel like work at all. I've never met anyone who created a Vision Statement and said they dreamed about a life that was a grind. So stop making it that way.

Small steps add up and begin to compound over time. Big, overwhelming steps where you make quick progress, then revert back and have to start over again don't.

Small steps are easy, so you're much more likely to do them. Small steps then become habits. When we're in the habit we no longer have to think about it, we just do it. It's like brushing your teeth. You don't have to set a goal to do it, you just do it.

Lower the bar, take small steps, build up momentum then confidence, begin creating healthy habits, and before long you'll see results that were fun to achieve. More fun = more joy.

Setting and achieving goals should not be overly complicated or too rigid. It's a recipe for failure. Instead, I suggest you flex and bend with your goals. Provided you are always headed in the direction of your ideal life, worry less about the system or timeframe and focus instead on your progress and success.

You can still do a monthly or quarterly check in. I certainly recommend this. But's it's truly more of a time to update and reflect on your progress, assess your achievements, pivot on any strategies falling short, celebrate wins, and feel good about yourself.

It should never be: "Another ninety days, another missed goal, and I still suck."

If you are tempted to feel bad about yourself, look back at your daily gratitude. Check out how many pages of your Momentum Grid got checked off. Flip back through your planner and look at all those tasks checked off. Relish how many times you stepped outside your comfort zone.

If you truly did the work, there is no way you can fail. You might not be at that final outcome—yet—but you should be much closer than you've ever been before.

The only way you will not see results is if you've skipped the exercises in this book, made excuses, snubbed the information, procrastinated everything, refused to make any changes, or given minimal effort to improvement. It's really that simple. You either did the work or you didn't.

Please do the work. Your life and joy are worth it.

To provide additional support, I've created a 10/3 Goal Strategy Worksheet. The 10/3 stands for 10 minutes, 3 times a day. It's breaking things down into super small steps but making sure those steps count. We can all find ten minutes three times a day to move our lives forward.

Here's how it works:

Use one worksheet for each of your goals. Keep in mind some goals are simple, and others more complex. When I say simple, it does not mean easy. Simple just means there are less steps involved to get to the end.

A more complex goal may have many moving parts, such as a big project for your business. One of my complex goals is to increase the Conversation Rate on my website by 2%. All the moving parts in a conversion rate include paid traffic, audience, copy, opt in rates, landing page, shopping cart, incentives, and more. Messing up in just one place can cause everything else after it not to perform as well. A goal like this will need to be broken down into smaller projects with plenty of strategy to ensure success.

The following areas are explained on the worksheet:

Step 1: Get Clear

This will tie into your Well-Being Assessment and Vision Statement. Score yourself for where you are now and what score you hope to achieve after the goal is complete.

Get your goal down to one clear, concise sentence and write it down.

List your desired outcomes from this goal. Spend time getting clear on what you're really trying to achieve. What are you really after?

You measure success by how well you have achieved your goal. For example, if you're trying to lose weight, how many pounds would that be? If you want more money in your savings account, how much money do you want to see there? Put a dollar figure on it. Every goal you set must be specific and measurable.

Once you achieve the goal, what's the outcome? Will you be able to finally fit back in your skinny jeans, have the money to purchase a much-needed new car, or repair a broken relationship? Whatever this is for you, write it down.

Step 2: Make a Plan

This is where the strategy begins. Answer each question openly and honestly and be prepared to do some additional work before starting the goal. Allow other thoughts and ideas to flow freely and take your time to think through the plan.

Step 3: Break It Down

Use this section to break the goal down into smaller projects. The more complex the goal, the more you want to really break it down into super small, manageable steps.

Step 4: Take Small Steps

Use these sheets to break the steps you'll need to take to complete each project down into ten-minute increments. Remember, just keep breaking it down further and further until you have a list of quick and easy steps to take. If a task will require twenty minutes to complete, no problem. It counts for two that day. Don't get crazy with this—keep it simple.

Step 5: Do The Work

The goal is three ten-minute actions each day (or more if you have time). Prioritize your actions before getting busy so you're not working each day from a massive, endless to do list.

Here's a simple system you can use to prioritize:

A = Push outside my comfort zone tasks

B = Important must do tasks

C = Do as you're able when time permits tasks

D = Delegate and don't do everything yourself tasks

E= Eliminate tasks that don't move me forward

Transfer items into *The Best Planner Ever* or daily planner of choice. Now you know how to work the system.

NOTE: You will not be able to predict everything that may happen during a goal. Your strategy may fail, and you need to revert to Plan B. Use the worksheet to go as deep as you can, but don't kill yourself trying to figure out every little detail. There may be projects you just need to start and see where they take you. Do the exercise as often as needed.

Cross things off the list. Don't be afraid to reassess weekly or monthly.

Things to know while breaking out your goals...

These general guidelines can be applied in a variety of ways but will also help shorten your curve and improve your success.

Be realistic. Don't sabotage yourself right out of the gate. Instead, challenge yourself just to the point of feeling a little fearful (that's good) but not so far that your mind knows it's totally unattainable (that's bad). *You should feel challenged and hopeful*—not like a failure before you even start.

Write them down. There is power in committing your goals to paper. It increases your chance of success. This is also why I encourage creating a written Vision Statement and Vision Board.

Set fewer goals overall. Looking at a huge list can make anybody want to stop before they start. Write all your goals down then narrow down the list to the top one to three things to accomplish. No more. When those are done, you can pick more.

It's okay to change! Life happens, things change, new information comes to us, we grow, we heal, and it affects our goals. Revisit your bigger goals every month and update them as necessary. *They are a work in progress, just like you,* so know they can change and adapt with you.

Hold yourself accountable. If you truly want to make a change and succeed, then surround yourself with people who will make you better and have your best interests at heart. Yes, that extra push can be uncomfortable, but accountability is truly what sets the most successful people apart from those who fail.

Strive for Balance. Over the course of fifty years, Gallup scientists conducted a global study of more than 150 countries giving an inside look into the well-being of more than 98% of the world's population. Five distinct factors emerged that represent the universal elements of well-being that differentiate a life that is thriving from one spent suffering. These five areas are:

- **CAREER**—How you occupy your time and doing the work you love.
- **LOVE**—Having strong relationships with your partner, family, friends, and love in your life.
- **MONEY**—Having enough money and effectively managing it with confidence.
- **HEALTH**—Good physical health, strong mind, and enough energy every day.
- **GIVE BACK**—Being engaged where you live, doing charitable works, and helping others step into greatness.

While 66% of people are doing well in at least one of these areas, *just 7% are thriving in all five.* Plus, when we struggle in one, it can damage our well-being and wear down our daily life. As we strengthen or improve our well-being in these areas, we live better every day.

Keep this in mind when setting goals. You don't have to have a goal in all five areas, but make sure you're truly happy and fulfilled in each area for optimal balance.

Emergency Action Plan

Sometimes even the best laid plans just go to hell. It happens to us all. The trick is in knowing (and being willing to admit) those areas where you tend to sabotage yourself and creating a new plan to follow.

We sabotage ourselves by getting just within reach of a goal and then get set back. We want a loving relationship and then have a big fight for no reason. We get on the scale, have lost weight, and then blow our diet. Our company finally turns a profit so we go buy a bunch of crap we don't really need and can't make payroll. Does any of this sound familiar?

This relates back to earlier chapters where I've discussed up-leveling your comfort zone. We are all preset with a level of success and happiness we think we deserve. This can be on a very subconscious level and we may not even be aware of it. As we start to get those things in life we really want, it feels different. Feeling different can be uncomfortable. When we're uncomfortable, we want to reset back to where we started.

As you start to set goals and get results you may experience discomfort. You may even unconsciously start to sabotage yourself. Try to be aware of what's really happening. It's almost like you have to reset your baseline of happiness. Move it up a notch.

Know that the discomfort is just part of the process. Embrace it, thank it, clear it, and send it on its way. Create an emergency action plan so when it hits, you have a plan and are prepared to deal with it.

10/3 Goal Strategy Worksheet

Step 1 | Get Clear

My Goal:

Type of Goal: ☐ Money ☐ Career ☐ Love ☐ Give Back ☐ Health

Score My Goal: Current Rating 1-10: _____ Desired Rating 1-10: _____

Timeframe to Complete:

Desired Outcome(s):

How It Will Feel To Accomplish This Goal:

How It's Measurable:

Step 2 | Make a Plan

What changes are required in my daily routine to be successful?

If I need time to complete this goal, what will I say no to or step away from to make the time?

What's the biggest obstacle I need to overcome?

Who can I surround myself with to help me succeed?

Are there any additional resources or education I need?

Do I need to eliminate any toxic places, people, or habits to succeed?

What actions do I need to take FIRST to clear the path for my goal to succeed?

Step 3 | Break it Down

Projects to Complete:

Project #1:

Project #2:

Project #3:

Project #4:

Project #5:

Step 4: Take Small Steps

Project #1

Tasks to Complete:

1. _____
2. _____
3. _____
4. _____
5. _____

Project #2

Tasks to Complete:

1. _____
2. _____
3. _____
4. _____
5. _____

Step 5 | Do the Work

Prioritize the tasks using the A, B, C, D, E system and transfer to a daily planner or organizer of your choice.

Summary

Strategy is just making a plan.

This is the part most people skip right over.

Taking the time to think through the "how" behind completing goals is key to success.

ELIMINATE OVERWHELM

"You can't calm the storm… so stop trying. What you can do is calm yourself. The storm will pass."
—Timber Hawkeye

OVERWHELM SUCKS. THAT'S why it gets its very own chapter in *The Joy Guide*. It presents itself in various forms including but not limited to:

- Tossing and turning for hours on end at night when you "should" be sleeping but your brain is on overdrive and you just can't fall asleep.

- Eating an entire pizza and gallon of ice cream by yourself because you have so much to do and cannot figure out what to do next, or any choice you make means someone will suffer, so you instead you stuff yourself silly and do nothing.

- Walking around all day feeling inside like a grenade about to explode at any minute.

- Forgetting to complete important tasks while busily finishing things that don't really matter at all.

You are not alone. In fact, most people these days are affected by overwhelm and stress in some way. According to Gallup on a scale of one to ten Americans rated their stress level at 4.9, which means most of us are living with a moderate amount of stress on a regular basis. Women are more likely than men to feel stress and reported an average of 5.3 versus 4.6 for men. Stress, overwhelm, and anxiety are causing a lot of sleepless nights, too. In fact, 70% of adults report their number one response to stress is losing sleep and 77% report overwhelming worry is causing a physical reaction in their body.

80% of people reported feeling stressed when at work and 40% classify their jobs as being extremely stressful. Workers who are stressed are more likely to come in late or call out sick. The total cost of stress to employers is around $300 billion. For the workers, 31% report stress on the job negatively affects their ability to maintain work life balance.

Are you more stressed now just reading this? I am. Oy.

Only one in seven reported living virtually stress free. What are they doing differently? They are taking steps to *manage* it. I don't know about you, but I want some of that. In today's world living is fast and furious. Unless you're existing in a bubble a truly tension free environment is pretty much impossible to attain. However, regardless of your life circumstance you can manage overwhelm, stress, and anxiety—if you choose to do so.

Some great ways to do this are any form of exercise you enjoy, meditation, taking things *off* your plate, and doing more activities that bring you joy. If your to do list is overflowing, and people are asking for more and more, it may cause such overload on your brain even thinking about scheduling time for these things it can send you deeper down the rabbit hole.

That's where the Brain Dump comes in to save the day. *Da-Dah-Dahhhhh!*

Your brain is a thinking device, not a storage device. The more you store up inside, the more likely you are to experience overwhelm. You've probably been there before. You have a ton of work to do, demands flying into your inbox, phone pinging away, no idea where to start, so you binge watch Netflix for twelve hours instead. Or the reverse: you start madly doing things on your list with no rhyme or reason until you drop from exhaustion and still feel like you got nothing accomplished.

The goal here is to create more joy in your life. It would be wonderful if overwhelm didn't occur, but it does and it will. The best defense is knowing how to handle it so you can move through it quickly and get back to working in the zone.

When you are in a state of overwhelm, your productivity suffers, your willpower goes flying out the window, your decision-making processes weakens, you feel like crap, and it just sucks. It's no way to live and cannot be part of your ideal joyful life.

Remember earlier when I talked about up-leveling your comfort zone of happiness? This is where it really applies. If you're used to working from a constant state of strain, you may actually wind up there on purpose because that's where you're comfortable. Moving through your day in a relaxed, confident, clear, focused state, may feel really weird and uncomfortable to you.

Just go with it. Try not to sabotage yourself. Work to shorten the times of feeling overwhelmed and lengthen the times of feeling clear and focused. Align with your Vision Statement. Did you dream about more peace, ease, joy, and flow in your life? Well, when it happens, hold on to it, put your claws into it, you are getting what you want.

Getting what you want can be exhilarating or terrifying. Sometimes both. Hold on to the joy and let the fear go. This is a choice only you can make. Choose the joy that comes from getting what you want.

If you aren't quite sure where to begin, I promised practical tools and tools you shall have! Here's an exercise to do anytime you feel overwhelmed. If you aren't feeling that way right now, it's okay. Do the exercise anyway. And keep it handy for any time stress hits, so you can get yourself out of it quick.

Doing this regularly will *prevent* overwhelm. It's a great weekly practice to boost all your decision-making processes around time management.

Here's how it works:

"Brain dump" everything in your head to paper. Don't worry about the order or about being neat and organized. Just get it all out of your head—work, personal issues, family, health, money, all of it. Write everything down to the tiniest detail on paper. Once you get it all out of your head, you should already be feeling clearer.

Next, go through everything on the list and prioritize it using the ABCDE system we learned earlier.

A = Top Priority

B = Important

C = Do As You Are Able

D = Delegate

E = Eliminate—Just say NO!

We'll dive deeper into the A task in the next chapter, but for now, just put an ABCD or E next to each item.

All your items *cannot* be an A. You must *eliminate* some of them. *Delegate* whenever possible. It does not all have to be done by you. Once the list is prioritized, you can then break down your As and Bs by A1, A2, A3, and so forth so you know the order in which you need to complete them.

The key to a successful brain dump is *prioritizing*. Without this, it's just creating a massive to do list that may stress you out more. There must be a sense of order to restore calm to your poor brain.

Finally, transfer the prioritized list to a clean sheet of paper that's now neat and organized into your daily planner of choice. Segment tasks each day so it's manageable and not further stress inducing. Doing this at the beginning of a new week will kick you off feeling *clear* and *focused*.

As new tasks arise in the course of a day, quickly place them where they go, (ABCDE) and get right back on track. You can also set a *time* for each task. For example, some tasks may take ten minutes and others an hour. When you assign a time to each task, it becomes even easier to pick out the one to do when you have a few minutes free.

For example, if I'm between client calls and I just have fifteen minutes, I can scan my list of A tasks and look for a ten-minute one. Knock it out quickly, and I'm back to work. Or, if it's the end of the day and I'm feeling a bit drained, I can find a few quick C tasks to get done. I'm still productive even though I don't have the brainpower for an A or B.

By now you're learning about my love of worksheets and tools so I've included one for the brain dump. Once you get into the habit of this practice it usually takes no more than 10-15 minutes. Benefits to doing this practice regularly include:

- It makes it easier to identify tasks that are low priority and where you can say no.

- It's a great *reminder* to delegate. Sometimes I just forget I have a team and get caught up in the "*Jennifer has to do everything herself show*" so a gentle nudge is a real blessing. We can do anything, but not everything (thank you David Allen for this quote) so delegate whenever possible.

- It enables you to plan out your A tasks so time is spent on things that will make a difference.

- You can group C tasks together and knock them out more efficiently.

- You'll end each day feeling more accomplished and satisfied with your progress.

- There is joy in feeling like you have your crap together.

If you truly want more pleasure, especially in your working life, this process is a must. Keeping yourself in a better state of mind will not only improve your mood, but also your productivity and decision-making skills. When you're in a better state of mind, it's just easier to keep the momentum going on your goals. This builds your confidence and keeps you feeling better and better.

Brain Dump ~ Prioritize ~ Organize

Brain Dump	Organize
	A - Push outside my comfort zone tasks
	B – Important must do tasks
	C – Do as I'm able and time permits tasks
	D – Delegate and don't do everything myself tasks
	E – Eliminate tasks that don't move me forward

Summary

Stress and overwhelm suck.

The people who live stress free do something to manage it.

Your brain is a thinking device, not a storage device.

Getting it out of your head and on to paper is good, but the difference comes when you prioritize.

You can do anything, but not everything—delegate.

It's okay to say no, so you can say yes
to the things that really matter.

THE LIFE CHANGING A TASK

> *"All your dreams can come true if you have the courage to pursue them."*
> —Walt Disney

It's deceptively simple how powerful the "A" task can be. If you've not taken time to understand and know your top priority each day, this alone could be the reason you're not succeeding at your goals, working more hours than necessary, and living without the kind of joy you dream about.

Let me explain…

In previous chapters we learned about the ABCDE system. When planning out the day and week using this system it becomes almost difficult *not* to have a clear grasp of where your time is going. You can even go back through past days in your schedule and see what you were working on. Did you spend time on easy C tasks just so you could cross more off your list and avoid the important A tasks, which would have moved your life forward?

No judgment! This is just about being more aware of where your time is being spent and intentionally directing it where you want it to go.

Let's look closer at the A task...

At first it may seem obvious these are the *important* things you must complete each day. It could be taking a client call, meeting with a vendor, a big sales presentation, or even picking the kids up from a special event—definitely all of these are important things. The problem is, *none* of them are your A task.

The A task is the action that takes you out of your comfort zone. It's the thing that might scare you a bit, you may be avoiding, but deep down in your heart you know it's what you should be doing to succeed.

- If you're a business owner, it could be making those outbound sales calls you have been dodging even though you're having cash flow issues and the extra revenue from those calls would be a blessing.
- It could be reaching out to some person or place and making a new connection that freaks you out. Or attending that networking event filled with prospective clients you've been avoiding.
- Maybe it's starting the process of looking for a new job, or steps to get out of a toxic relationship.
- Maybe it's taking the leap to sign up with a business or life coach, look for a therapist, or attend a conference out of town.

The A task moves the needle. It's the catalyst for success. It is not the client/patient/vendor/employee/ customer/

school visit you're going to do anyway. Those are important, of course, but they're the B tasks for the day.

The A task often takes less than thirty minutes a day. It does not have to take up some crazy amount of time. Sometimes it's as simple as sending an email or making just one phone call. It can be broken into three ten-minute actions or two fifteen-minute actions. It's designed to be those few special things you do each day to move closer to your ideal life.

The A task requires you to *push*.

Push forward to what you really want. Do not stop when you're tired. Stop when you're done. Tap deep into yourself and go for it.

Looking back on my life, when I was in my darkest hour, my A task was hiring a life coach to help me. At that time, I was alone with three children, working a full-time job, and despite the fact I made great money, I lived check to check. I had my initial free consult call with the coach and desperately wanted to hire her. I had $900 in my savings account. Her fee was $900 to the penny.

I worried I was being selfish and irresponsible for draining my entire savings account to spend on myself. The list of "what ifs" raced through my mind…

What if I needed that money for some emergency for my kids?

What if the coaching didn't work?

What if people found out what I did?

What if I was wrong about this?

I was scared shitless.

So I did it.

Then I showed up 100% to our calls. I was honest. I was vulnerable. When she suggested different exercises for me, like getting clear on my Core Values and creating a Vision Statement for my life, I took it to heart and did the work. I was working eleven-hour days at a corporate nightmare job and raising three kids by myself. I didn't make excuses. I made the time and got it done.

This was *before* I knew about the ABCDE system. It was just a step I was scared to take, but in my heart I knew it was the right thing. I knew the best I could do for my children was to heal myself. If I could have done it on my own, I would have. I needed help. It was key to moving forward.

Before I hired the coach, my A task was accepting an invitation to a women's networking meeting I normally never would have attended. Then my push became going to the meeting each week. Then it was practicing the meditation technique I learned even though it felt awkward. Taking these initial steps led me to hiring the coach.

If I had not found the courage to take those steps, which were scary and uncomfortable, I'm afraid to think where I would be today. What I discovered in the darkest hours of my life is when you take a frightening step forward, it opens a door. Not all doors lead somewhere, but enough of them do to change your life.

As one door opens, it leads you to another, then another. When I was suffering daily, living in a functional depression and the only thing keeping me alive was the thought of what my children would do without me, I could not see the chain of events that began to unfold with the first step of opening up to a co-worker when she asked me if I was okay and I broke down crying at her desk. The weight of it all was just too heavy to carry any longer.

Here I was this big shot senior female executive making a six-figure income and living in Fort Lauderdale, which I admit looked pretty sweet on paper. But the reality was I had no extended family or friends close by, an abusive ex who was terrorizing me, no extra money in the bank. I was still in enormous debt from a previous failed business. When my two horses died within thirty days of each other, it broke me.

I could not see at that time the joy that would eventually come into my life. I did not realize how each step started me down a new path, a new life. Looking back now I can see it clearly.

Going through the motions and surviving each day never letting on how much I was struggling. Thankfully a co-worker noticed I wasn't myself. She took weeks to get up the courage to ask me if I was okay. When she finally did, instead of pretending I was fine, I confessed I was not and stood crying at her desk.

This led to me finding out she ran a women's empowerment group in the evenings. She was a front desk receptionist, but her dream was empowering women. She invited me to her group, and I went. This led to making friends who provided me with support, which led to hiring a coach.

The coach helped me process through the grief and pain and begin creating a new life for myself. This led to leaving corporate and moving to North Carolina to live with my sister for the summer. It was the first summer I didn't work since I was ten years old. I needed time to heal and I took it.

This led to starting my consulting practice and stepping back out on my own. Corporate was not for me and I wanted to be present for my children. I knew this now.

This led to me be being introduced (by the coach I hired) to the man I'm married to today. It was two years after we had worked together. Out of the blue she calls me. "There's a great guy I want you to meet. He needs some help marketing his books. Plus, he's single."

At this time, I had zero desire to get hooked up. I told her very clearly, I would help with his marketing but nothing further.

She gave me his number and then proceeded to harass me until I called him. Which I did and turned out she gave me the wrong number. I left a message for someone who sounded like a creeper and hoped that would be the end of it.

A few days later my phone rang. It was a New York number I didn't recognize. Normally I would never answer this type of call but for some reason this day, I picked up. It was the guy. My coach had given him my number and insisted he call me.

We hit it off instantly. He asked me on a phone date that night and we talked straight through until dawn. In the early morning hours, he said, "Well, we've covered pretty much everything. I guess the only thing left is will you marry me?" I said, "Hell yes." Two years later we made it official and were married at the top of a mountain surrounded by our closet family and friends.

We relocated to upstate New York where I knew nobody. My husband had family and friends—he is originally from

New York—but I was starting from scratch. I started a local Meet Up group to make some connections. Scary? Nerve wracking? Uncomfortable? Oh hell yes. All of the above. But I met one of my best friends there. I've long since stopped the group, but if I'd never put it out there with that A task, I would not have met her.

The A tasks were not done with me. From there I signed up to attend a networking group in the city. I had researched them online but was terrified to join that first meeting. It required me to take the train into New York City all by myself. I wasn't raised in a "train" town, so all the schedules and routes were confusing. I'd pop out of the subway and have no idea what direction to head in. But I did it. When I was there, I met the founder and gave her my business card (another scary action). A few weeks later she offered me a position in the company, and I ended up becoming their President and tripling revenues.

This only happened because of the A task. I wanted to chickenshit out, more than anything, but I didn't. I stepped outside my comfort zone and big things happened. As I stepped outside the box more often and realized I wouldn't die and the world kept spinning, I gained the courage to do it again and again and again. Today, when I feel fear around taking any step forward, that's my cue to go for it.

When you've been to hell and survived, things can still be scary, but you have the courage to know what doesn't kill you does in fact make you stronger.

Please understand, every A task won't lead to some giant cosmic success. Many of mine went nowhere and success didn't happen overnight. The idea is to get clear on what your

A task is and then go do it. Now you've done your part. It opens the door for good things to enter and closes the door on what you no longer desire. But nothing happens until you take that first step.

I used to believe planning my day was sitting, ass in the chair, and making a giant to do list. This is not planning; it's making a list. Now I spend time in quiet meditation, clear any junk holding me back, journal, read and align with my Vision Statement, check in with my goals, then ask myself "what action will move me closer?" This action becomes my A task for the day, and everything else gets done around it. The shorter my list for the day, the better.

If it's uncomfortable, good. If it scares me a little, even better. Life doesn't happen while hiding or making excuses. There is joy in trying.

Depending on where you are the A task might be to set a boundary. Or perhaps make time for self-care. It could be to change a belief, stop beating yourself up, or do the exercises in this book. A top task could be to get more sleep, so you have the energy to look for a new job. Perhaps it's journaling through the fear around writing down your dream life in a Vision Statement. It could be asking for help or admitting you're wrong.

The A task is a step in a new direction. Sometimes it will be that cold email pitch that landed the big meeting and changed your business forever. Or answering a phone call that leads to finding the love of your life. Your step might feel big, or it might feel small. It's your step. Own it and take it from wherever you are.

Now you know what an A task should be. Take a closer look at your daily to do list. Are there items on there you've marked as As which are actually Bs or Cs? Are there actions you're procrastinating out of fear? Is there something in your heart you want to do but are making excuses and keep putting it off?

Just do it. If it's something big, break it down into smaller steps. Take one step each day.

When you go to bed at night, you'll know you did something to move the needle. You'll feel like you're operating at a much higher level, and while it might still be a little scary, you'll be eager to get up and do it again the next day.

This is your personal power starting to flow, and it should feel pretty fantastic. Don't fight it. Let it go and enjoy the ride. There is joy outside your comfort zone.

Summary

Know and understand what an A task is.

Push yourself to complete at least one daily.

THE DAILY PLANNING HABIT

"Plans are nothing; planning is everything."
—Dwight D. Eisenhower

To BE INTENTIONAL with time, so your results are maximized, requires preparation and planning. When you first begin doing this, it may take longer than you're used to. As you build and master the habit, it can be done in a quick five to ten minutes each day.

I could go on for pages trying to convince non-believers in the daily planning habit. But there's just no way around this one. If you launch into the day without thought or focus, you will be busier than you need to be. That will leave you with less time to enjoy life. It will be harder and take longer to meet your goals.

PLANNING IS NOT JUST MAKING A LIST.

To be effective at planning, *not* list making, requires time and thought.

However, if you take the time to get clear on what you want your life to look like, map out a strategy to get there, identify your priority tasks each day and do them, you will achieve the life you dream about.

When you get off track—and because life happens you will—you'll be able to get back on very quickly. Because you've done the pre-planning work, you may find you get off track far less than before—maybe not at all.

Going into the day clear and focused reduces your stress level. You may even find your work is more enjoyable because your effort goes farther. You can end each day feeling accomplished knowing you got the most important things done. It's so much more fun to watch your goals unfold with ease than running in circles and hoping you might get there. If any part of your strategy doesn't work as intended, you simply pivot in a new direction.

As you perfect this process you may start finding more time for yourself, room in your schedule that wasn't there before. This is good! Don't rush to fill it with "stuff." In the beginning you may be so in the habit of filling every minute of the day with work, it might feel weird to have some gaps.

Remember, we are here to find and live your joy. Do you work every minute in your ideal life? Probably not. So when you start to receive the gift of more time, accept it and say, "Thank you."

It's so sweet to start getting what you want. The trick is to accept it. Then keep planning for more!

Let's take a look at the elements of a strong daily planning habit:

Read Your Vision Statement

Align with the direction of your life, first. When you're clear on the outcome, it's easier to take steps to achieve it today. Study your Vision Board. See yourself being successful. Journal. Meditate. Live in alignment with your values.

Identify Your A Tasks

Refer to your Goals and strategy sheet. You've done the work to think through the "how" behind achieving your goals so identify the top A tasks for the day and transfer them into your daily planner of choice. Push outside your comfort zone. Delete and clear any limiting beliefs or excuses.

Line out B and C Tasks

This is the normal scheduling you do now, except organize things on your list into higher and lower priority. This prevents you from having a day filled with C stuff and never moving forward on your goals.

Delegate / Follow Up

Delegate tasks to others. This could be to employees, contractors, vendors, peers, or even your kids. Once a task is delegated, you may still need to follow up. You don't want to assign it out and have it fall through the cracks. Delegate and follow up as necessary.

Self-Care

Self-care should become a normal and natural part of your day. A good habit you practice. Write down what you'll do to take care of yourself and do it.

Nutrition Tracking

Plan out the nutrition and movement you'll add to your day to fuel your body and give you the energy needed to live each day to the fullest.

Notice how these small steps will lead to a truly effective daily plan. It will take work to get clear on your vison and map out the strategy behind goals. Once this is done, however, it saves time each day because now the effort takes you farther, faster. There is joy in being effective.

Summary

Making a list is not planning.

To be effective each day requires time and thought.

The work of creating a Vision Statement and goal strategy pays off in less time executing each day.

ME TIME IS NONNEGOTIABLE

"The relationship with yourself sets the tone for every other relationship you have."

—Jane Travis

After I relocated to New York and attended that first scary networking meeting, a short time later I was asked by the founder to lead their national network of women entrepreneurs. When I first started with the company, they offered a daily action plan to follow. I was to not only use this design for myself but teach it to others.

One of the items on this daily plan was taking time to celebrate, enjoy life, and have fun.

I was in my early 40s at this time and in my entire professional career I'd never put anything on a to do list that was fun. The concept was lost on me. Sad, right? I made lists to get stuff *done*. Even a list around a vacation was all the things I needed to do to get ready for it and catch up after it. I did not make lists to waste time relaxing and pampering myself.

The idea blew my mind. Only when I started to put this into practice did I begin to see the true power of it.

Taking time for myself was never something I learned as a child. I had three younger sisters, and with both my parents working two jobs each, the responsibility of caring for them often fell on my shoulders. I had my first full-time job in the summers when I was ten. I've had either a job or business (sometimes both) ever since then.

Responsibility and work ethic have always come before fun. As I grew older, it became apparent that all work and no play made Jennifer very tired, cranky, and unhappy. I found myself asking, "Why am I working so hard for no real reward here?"

I had my wires crossed. I was working hard so I could relax and have fun, but because I was in the habit of always working hard, putting the needs of others before my own and people pleasing, I never developed the skill of being able to let go and enjoy. It is a talent, too. For those of us who have a hard time saying no or feel guilty when we do, this takes practice to master.

The good news is if I can get this down, so can you. When you do, the results are astounding. You can still work hard and really enjoy it. You can also play hard and really enjoy that, too. Sometimes I find myself napping hard on the couch, without feeling the least bit guilty, and that's fun like you cannot believe.

Taking care of yourself is essential and no longer optional in a joyful life. You are doing those around you a disservice by running yourself into the ground. Do you really think the people in your life who truly love you really want you to hurt yourself for their benefit? If the answer is yes, then it's time to take a hard look at the people in your life.

As a mother, I would never want my child to hurt him or herself to please me. Think about your best friend. Do they withhold their friendship if you're not bending over backwards for them? A true friend would not.

It's time to start being our own best friend, putting our needs and feelings first. It's not a license to be a selfish, self-centered jerk, but an empowered person who values their well-being so they *can* love those around them to the best of their abilities.

For some of you, taking care of yourself may feel a little foreign. If you're a people pleaser, it may feel downright uncomfortable. But let's take a moment to reflect upon the picture of your ideal life. Are you running around all day keeping everybody else happy and ignoring your own needs to the point of exhaustion and burnout? I hope not. Instead, you're more likely surrounded by loving people and healthy relationships, including a healthy relationship with yourself. You're taking time to do the things you love, pursue hobbies, playing music, creating art, being out in nature, feeling great, and loving every minute of your life.

It may prove quite difficult to go from never taking care of yourself to putting your own needs first, quickly. Instead, like everything else we've done in this guide, ease into it. You certainly recognize the value of self-care. The next step is to start living it.

Daily self-care is critical to keep your own battery fully charged. When you're charged up, you'll work better, be more productive, and have a lot more fun, too. If you find yourself feeling guilty for taking time for yourself, use this two-word statement: **I MATTER**. Say it as many times as necessary to stop guilt in its tracks and get back to taking amazing care of you.

If you have put self-care on the back burner for so long you have no clue what to do to take care of yourself, that's okay... this is a time to explore, experiment, and rediscover yourself.

Think back throughout your life and make a list of the things you enjoyed doing in the past. Consider friends or family members and how they live their joy. Is there someone you look up to? What hobbies or interests do they pursue that get your heart pumping?

Make a list of these things and you can even break it down into time increments. For example, a quick pick me up might be a ten-minute meditation or stretch or sit outside in the sunshine. When time permits it may be a two-hour hike, or ten-mile bike ride, or lazy day on the couch with a good book.

Making a list ahead of time takes the guesswork out of figuring out what to do when you have a block of time. This way you can just scan the list, grab something you love, and off you go. Every single day strive to do at least one thing for yourself (even if it's just ten minutes).

NOTE: Once you start doing this, don't be surprised if you find yourself getting territorial over this time. When I don't get the opportunity to care for myself each day, I can get cranky. I'll find my husband saying things to me like, "Hey, don't you want to go out for your walk?" or "When was the last time you were at the barn?" Even he has come to recognize I'm a much better person to be around when I've cared for my own needs.

This is a *fun* exercise, so have fun with it. Just start with ten minutes a day and work your way up from there! This is joy in taking care of yourself.

Self-Care Actions

Time Required	Things that make me feel good and recharge my batteries:

Summary

Taking care of our own needs is nonnegotiable.

You are doing your loved ones a disservice by running yourself into the ground.

If you don't know how to care for yourself, this is an opportunity to explore and figure it out.

Planning for self-care will ensure it gets done, like any other important task.

PUTTING IT ALL TOGETHER

"It's not the circumstances that create joy, it's you."
—Unknown

WE'VE BEEN ON quite the journey together and the final step is to pull everything together in a simple, repeatable, predictable process you can follow each day. That does not mean every day will be the same, but it does mean you will be prepared for whatever life brings.

To find and live your joy—despite any and all crap going on in the world—requires a commitment. It's a decision and a choice only *you* can make. When you make the choice to let your joy out of its cage, you might get kicked around a bit. There may be challenges that present, or people in your life who don't want you to change. It might be hard, and you may even want to give up. Please don't. Stick to your guns on this one, it's worth the effort.

I've outlined simple systems you can use to implement the fundamentals in this guide, including a Joy Finder Cheat Sheet when the shit hits the fan and you're not sure which tool to use.

Make it yours. Change what you need to work for you, just don't lose sight of the purpose behind the tool or exercise.

PLANNING

Daily

- Get Connected and Quiet. Clear any Crap. Journal. (5-15 minutes)
- Read and Align with Your Vision Statement/Vision Board (2-3 minutes)*
- Sit with your Focus Wheel (1 minute)*
- Practice Gratitude (5 minutes)
- Schedule Self Care (1 minute)
- Identify Your A Tasks (1 minute)*
- Keep Bs and Cs Where They Belong (5 minutes)
- Plan your nutrition (1 minute)
- Delegate whenever possible (2 minutes)
- Say no, frequently, to low priority tasks and time wasters

Once you've done the work to complete a Vision Statement, Focus Wheel, and mapped out your Goal Strategy these items take very little time each day. Set aside at least 1-2 hours initially to complete. You can also use the L.I.G.H.T your day practice found in the Best Journal Ever.

Weekly

- Weekly Reflection (5-10 minutes)
- Plan Meals (10 minutes)
- Identify A Tasks for the Week (5-10 minutes)
- Clean Up—go back through the past week in your planner of choice and identify anything that didn't get done and carry it forward (5-10 minutes)

Monthly

- Reflect and update your Well-Being Assessment Scores (10 minutes)
- Reflect and update your Vision Statement and Vision Board (10 minutes)
- Map out goal strategy (30 minutes)

Yearly

- Create or update Vision Statement & Vision Board (1-2 Hours)
- Outline Goals for the Year (1-2 Hours)
- Take time to reflect on progress and accomplishments (30 minutes)

MINDSET

Here's a simple practice I created using the acronym L.I.G.H.T. It helps me easily remember the key elements each day to keep my mindset in tip-top shape. Use this practice like a dial. On days where you have more time, dial it up. On days where time is tight, dial it down. Just try not to turn the dial off. You can also break up the components and do them throughout the day at any time that makes sense for you.

- **Let go of the crap**—this is twenty minutes of *journaling* to let go of any negative emotions or dark feelings to clear your emotional system and prepare it for healthy, vibrant, life force energy to flow freely.

- **Ignite your power**—once you've cleared the ick do something to ignite your power such as *meditation* or *movement*. Ideally shoot for twenty minutes here, but again, depending on your life and day you can dial it up or down. Connect yourself with any higher power of your choosing to feel radiant, grounded, and in your heart.

- **Give thanks**—this is a daily *gratitude practice* in any form that suits. You can offer free flowing thoughts about people, places, things for which you are grateful. You might list 3-5 things you are grateful for and why.

- **Hold your vision**—if you've created a Vision Statement, read and connect to it daily. Spend a few minutes visualizing it actually happening. See yourself being successful in all things.

- **Take action**—finally, this is where you choose the next action steps to get you closer to the vision. Take action from a place of connection and insight, instead of just leaping into another busy day running around with your hair on fire.

JOY FINDER CHEAT SHEET

I'm so super stuck on a goal	**Journal** out the emotions behind feeling stuck. Let it rip for 20 minutes to clear your thinking or identify limiting beliefs blocking you. Reprogram them with a **Clearing Statement**. Then, create a **Momentum Grid**. Lower the bar so far you cannot fail. Start taking baby steps each day until momentum and confidence return.
I feel so overwhelmed	**Brain Dump** it all out of your head and then organize and prioritize. When you get it out of your head, you'll be able to think clearly again. Repeat as often as necessary. If you continue the pattern of constantly being overwhelmed, **Journal** about it daily. Ask the questions "What would it take for me to stop taking on so much?" or "What would it take for me to start saying no?" and let your thoughts flow freely. Follow your heart on the page and see where it goes without judgement.

My mindset is really negative

You can do one or all of these—just choose what feel best for you...

Take 15-20 minutes each day of **Quiet Time** to clear anything blocking your mindset or keeping you stuck.

Begin a daily **Gratitude Practice**. Start with 10 minutes a day and intentionally look for all the things in your life to be grateful for and why. Write them down. Look back on past days' gratitude and *feel* grateful in your heart. Ask the question "What can I learn from this situation?" and work to pull the good from it.

Create a **Focus Wheel** and sit with it when you need a lift or just because it feels good.

Write **Affirmations** in places you can see them. You can find a list of them at the end of this book.

Journal daily before doing any mindset work to clear negative emotion. If you're in a bad place, that's fine. Let yourself feel whatever negative emotions are coming up and release them on the pages. Once you feel more clear, then do something positive to reset like **Affirmations** or **Focus Wheel**. While journaling you can also ask the question "What's blocking my joy?" or "Why am I afraid to be in a happy place?" and see what comes up for you.

I feel like I'm going in a million directions	Read your **Vision Statement** and reconnect with the direction of your life. Look at the list of things you're doing each day and remove anything not in alignment. Use a **Time Affirmation** to reprogram your thinking. If you constantly tell the story "I am always going in a million directions" then you will always be going in a million directions. Begin to replace this with a new belief such as "I am clear, focused, and organized".
My brain hurts, I can't think anymore	Take 10-20 minutes of **Quiet Time** daily to sit and breathe. Use a guided meditation if that's easier for you. Clear your mind and allow your brain to rest. To quiet the mind, you may need to do a **Brain Dump** and then sit quietly. You may need to sit quietly and then Brain Dump so you release things as they come up. **Journal** for 20 minutes on any anger, frustration, or disappointment you feel around your head being so clouded. Make sure you're adding enough **Nutrition** to your diet. Plenty of live raw foods to help clear the mind and eliminate foggy brain. Use your **Daily Planning Sheet** as a reminder to add nutrition or movement to help you clear and feel grounded again.

I am so beat down and worn out

Self care, self care, self care—stop making excuses and do something for yourself.

Take a nap or set time aside to sleep in.

Eat a salad or drink a raw green juice.

Get some movement (whatever works best for you) such as going for a run or doing light yoga, but only if this helps you recharge. Make sure exercise doesn't add to your exhaustion. If you need to, rest first then move.

Use a **Time Affirmation** and take control of your schedule. Move things back to later or simply say no to some projects to give yourself space.

Take a weekend away at your favorite destination and use the time to rest, recharge, relax, and sit quietly. If you find yourself making excuses like you don't have the time or money, push back and set a positive intention. You have the power to make it happen if you choose to do so.

Schedule a large block of time for an activity you love such as gardening, reading, walking, or napping.

Journal around the exhaustion. What led up to you feeling this way? How does it feel? How can you let yourself relax? Is there a limiting belief here you need to reprogram? Be gentle with yourself but seek answers.

I feel like there are never enough hours in a day	Reprogram your thinking using a **Time Affirmation**. Write it, think it, speak it, live it, and you *will* make more time in your life. Use the ABCDE system when planning your day. Make sure time is going to the *right* things each day.
I'm not feeling much joy	Begin keeping a **Joy Journal**. As you move through the day, intentionally look for things that bring you joy and write them down. At the end of each day review the list and allow yourself to feel great. Use an **Affirmation** around joy such as: My day begins and ends with gratitude and joy. I am guided to an abundance of joy. Joy flows through me. I attract joy into my life. Today I am brimming with energy and overflowing with joy.

AFFIRMATIONS

TIME

Because my day is organized, I am always on time for every appointment I make.

I have plenty of time for everything.

I am well-organized and always on time.

Being in control of my time energizes me.

I appreciate that time is as valuable as money, thus I use every minute wisely.

Being organized gives me more time to do the things I want.

I continually improve my time management skills.

Being organized saves me so much time.

I control how I spend my time.

Every day I do more things in less time.

I create prioritized to do lists and follow them through.

Every day I make more time for the things I love.

I decide when, where, and how I spend my time.

Every minute of my day is dynamic and productive.

I do what needs to be done, when it needs doing.

Every morning I make a to do list and follow it throughout the day.

I easily resist the temptation to work on low priority tasks.

I always clear all the items on my daily to do list.

I enjoy arriving ahead of schedule.

I always do the right things at the right time.

I ensure that I always arrive at work at least fifteen minutes early.

I always have plenty of time to do what I want to do.

I always make time for the things I want in life.

I ensure that I am always doing the most important task for this moment.

I always manage my time effectively.

I always use my time wisely.

I get tasks done in a timely manner.

I am an excellent time manager.

I get things done on time.

I am committed to managing my time effectively.

I get things done quickly and efficiently.

I am in control of my time and my life.

I give myself time to do each task at perfect speed.

I am making time in my life to…

I have a great respect for other people's time.

I am making time today to…

I have absolute control over my time.

MONEY

I am a magnet for money. Prosperity is drawn to me.

Money comes to me in expected and unexpected ways.

I move from poverty thinking to abundance thinking.

I am worthy and deserve to make more money.

I am open and receptive to all the wealth life offers me.

I embrace all new avenues of income.

I welcome an unlimited source of income and wealth in my life.

I release all negative energy over money.

Money comes to me easily and effortlessly.

I use money to better my life and the lives of others.

Wealth constantly flows into my life.

My actions create constant prosperity.

I am aligned with the energy of abundance.

I constantly attract opportunities that create more money.

My finances improve beyond my dreams.

Money is the root of joy and comfort.

Money and spirituality can co-exist in harmony.

Money and love can be friends.

Money is my servant.

I am the master of my wealth.

I am able to handle large sums of money.

I am at peace with having a lot of money.

I can handle massive success with grace.

Money expands my life's opportunities and experiences.

Money creates joy in my life.

I love money and it loves me.

LOVE

All of my relationships offer a positive, loving experience.

I am worthy of love and deserve to receive love in abundance.

I love those around me and I love myself.

I attract loving and caring people into my life.

My partner and I are both happy and in love. Our relationship is joyous.

I am thankful for the love in my life and I am thankful for my caring partner.

I only attract healthy, loving relationships.

I am with the love of my life. We both treat each other with respect.

I happily give and receive love each day.

I am so thankful for my partner and how caring they are.

Each day I am so grateful for how loved I am.

I know and trust that the Universe will only bring me loyal supporting and loving relationships.

I open my heart to love and know that I deserve it.

Wherever I go and whoever I am with, I find love.

I deserve to receive the love I get, and I open myself to the love the Universe gives me.

I am open to marriage and attracting my future spouse.

My love (and/or marriage) grows stronger every day.

I am capable and deserving of a long-lasting relationship.

My relationship will be open, honest and full of abundance.

Love surrounds me and everyone around me.

I am attracting my dream future.

I am confident, self-assured and full of joy.

I exhale negativity and inhale happiness.

Today I will continue to create the foundation of a happy and loving relationship.

I love myself fully and completely.

Today I will attract love and happiness.

My relationships are always fulfilling.

Happiness begins with me and me alone. I have the power to create my own happiness.

I let go of my past relationships and look to the future.

I only think positively about love.

JOY

I choose to be joyful.

I live with joy.

My life is full of joy.

I spread joy with every step I take on my journey.

I give joy to others.

I will go with the flow; my life is easy and filled with joy.

I look at the world with the eyes of joy.

I radiate joy.

I am surrounded by joy.

Joy is in my heart and in my life.

I am joy.

I will create a life full of joy and peace.

I wake up every morning to love and joy.

I accept peace and joy in all aspects of my life.

Joy is a healing choice and I choose it for myself now.

I am organized and have a home full of joy and peace.

I release all anxiety, fear, doubt, and worry to the power within me and I am filled with love, peace, and joy.

Joyful dreams of love surround me everywhere.

Weekly Reflection Questions

Take time each week to sit quietly and reflect. You can choose items to reflect on or pick from this list of questions. You can answer as many as you choose each week. Don't be afraid to mix it up and make it yours.

What am I really proud of?

How did I learn or improve?

What am I grateful for?

In what area of my life do I need to feel better?

Am I allowing my goals to unfold naturally with ease?

Are my thoughts in alignment with my higher self?

Is there anything I'm not getting done or actively avoiding?

What's one action I could take this week to get back on track?

What surprised me this week?

What is the biggest insight I received?

What unhealthy habit will I work to replace this week?

How can this help me move closer to living my best life?

How committed am I to healing my crap?

What is blocking me?

What lies or limiting beliefs do I need to delete and re-program?

Additional Tools and Resources

- *Best Planner Ever*—Daily planner I developed around the principles in this book.
- *Best Journal Ever*—Daily journal where the pages are designed to be ripped out and destroyed. Follows the LIGHT your day mindset practice.
- Online Courses—You'll find printable versions of all the worksheets and exercises in this book in our online courses. *www.BestPlannerEver.com*
- Private Coaching—if you need personalized coaching to help you through the principles in this book. *www.JenniferDawnCoaching.com*

FINAL THOUGHTS…

Savor the joyful moments in each day. Celebrate little wins as you watch your goals unfold. Laugh often at yourself. Let everything go. Fulfill your life purpose and be happy.

Time to let your joy loose.

That's it for now…

—Jennifer

Made in the USA
Monee, IL
08 November 2023